PROTEST IN MODERN SPAIN

The Struggle for Religious Pluralism

Dale G. Vought

William Carey Library

SOUTH PASADENA, CALIF.

P. H. WELSHIMER MEMORIAL LIBRARY
MILLIGAN COLLEGE
MILLIGAN COLLEGE, TENN. 37682

BX
4851
.V68

© Copyright 1973 by Dale G. Vought

All rights reserved. No part of this book may be used or reproduced in any manner whatsoever without written permission, except in the case of brief quotations embodied in critical articles or reviews. For information address the William Carey Library.

Library of Congress Cataloging in Publication Data

Vought, Dale G   1937
   Protestants in modern Spain

   Originally presented as the author's thesis
(MA in Missions), Fuller Theological Seminary.
   Bibliography: p.
   1. Protestants in Spain. 2. Protestant churches--Spain.
   I. Title.
BX4851.V68 1973   280'.4'0946   73-9744
ISBN 0-87808-311-1
                                        4/74

In accord with some of the most recent thinking in the academic press, the William Carey Library is pleased to present this scholarly book which has been prepared from an author-edited and author-prepared camera-ready manuscript.

Published by the William Carey Library
305 Pasadena Avenue
South Pasadena, Calif. 91030
Telephone: 213-799-4559

PRINTED IN THE UNITED STATES OF AMERICA

Contents

72195

Figures

Terms

The following is an explanation of the way in which particular words have been used in this study.

Church - When the word "church" is used to refer to the Evangelical Church or the Catholic Church in general, it will be with a capital. In lower case it refers to a local congregation.

Church Growth - In all cases when church growth is mentioned, it is in reference to the addition of church members.

Evangelical - The word "Evangelical" is used when referring to the Protestant Church in general. It is used in Spain by all non-Catholic groups regardless of denomination or background. It is preferred to the controversial word "Protestant." In the plural it refers to all Protestants.

Expansion growth - The growth of a local church which does not involve the beginning of new churches is referred to as expansion growth.

Extension growth - When local churches begin other churches, it is referred to as extension growth.

Mission - The word "mission" is used to refer to a sending church, denominational mission board, an interdenominational faith mission, an organization of missionaries on the field, or, in some cases, the task of the church. The context should make the meaning clear in each case.

Protestant - The words "Protestant" and "Evangelical" are used interchangeably and refer generally to the non-Catholic population of Spain.

Abbreviations

E.F.M.C.C. - Evangelical Foreign Missions Consultation
Committee.

F.I.E.I.D.E. - La Federación de Iglesias Evangélicas
Independientes de España.

G.B.U. - Grupo Bíblico Universitario.

H.O.A.C. - Hermandades Obreras de Acción Católica.

J.O.C. - Young peoples part of H.O.A.C.

I.E.E. - Iglesia Evangélica de España.

I.E.R.E. - Iglesia Española Reformada Episcopal.

U.E.B.E. - Unión Evangélica Bautista Española.

Preface

Spain has aroused the interest of the world in recent years. Its sunny beaches attract over twenty-eight million tourists a years to enjoy some of the most modern facilities in Europe. Its low prices have encouraged industry and commerce to invest large quantities of money and energy into the economy, making it one of the most stable in the world. Shaking off the shackles of isolation and indifference, Spain has finally joined the twentieth century. No longer walled isolation, but world involvement is the cry of the new generation.

There are recorded in the pages of the history of this noble country, now and again, references to a small but significant group of people. That group is the subject of this study. Most often they are referred to as the "Protestants" or preferably - The Evangelical Church of Spain. There is a need to emphasize that the Evangelical Church does exist and that it is growing in Spain. A description of this growth, and the conditions that govern it are crucial to the understanding of this portion of the body of Christ.

It is not enough to say that a group of some thirty thousand Evangelical Christians exist within a society of thirty-four million people unless there is some understanding of how they exist. Important issues face that Church today and those issues must be faced with understanding. An immense task of evangelization lies before the Church if the men and women of Spain are to have the option of a living, vital, personal relationship with Jesus Christ presented to them.

Good studies of the Evangelical Church in Spain have been
done in the past. The book of García and Grubb, done in 1933,
is an excellent work, but the Civil War of 1936-1939 changed
the situation completely. More recently there have been other
studies of value, but they have all preceded the passing of
the Law of Religious Liberty and again the situation has been
drastically changed. To give an up-to-date picture of the
Protestant Church in Spain is the reason for this study. It
is hoped that the reader will come to a deeper understanding
of the situation of the Protestants and a deeper appreciation
for their struggle in the development of a new religious tradition.

The abundance of reliable information on the early history
of the Evangelicals makes it unnecessary for me to repeat that
history in this study. The bibliography is not complete and
comprehensive, but it will be of help to those who might care
to read more on the subject. Because of the materials already
available to those who care to read on the Evangelical Church
prior to 1940, this study has its emphasis on the more recent
developments that have affected the Evangelicals of Spain.

Having worked in Spain for a period of four and one half
years with an Evangelical Church, I have had the opportunity
to see the situation firsthand. It is recognized however, that
there are definite limitations to what is presented here and
that it is in no way to be considered the "final word." My
fellow laborers will find occasion to make additions and cor-
rections. I trust that they will do so. Perhaps it will
serve to inspire someone to do an in-depth study of the growth
of the Evangelical Church in Spain. The lack of such a work
at the present time has prompted this effort to bridge the gap.

The preparation has involved consultations with many people,
the reading of many related books, articles, reports, and the
sending of two questionnaires. One questionnaire was sent to
the churches of Spain and the other was sent to the missionaries
working in Spain at that time. The questionnaires were sent out
in the spring of 1971 in anticipation of my studies at the School
of World Mission in Pasadena, California. The lack of a sufficient number of churches responding to the questionnaire made
that source of information of little value for the purposes of

this study. A personal visit would be necessary to obtain the
detailed information needed for a comprehensive study of church
growth. The general impressions received by study of the questionnaires that were answered did help in the understanding of
trends and patterns in the Evangelical Church. The good response of the missionaries was also helpful. Anticipating my
need for materials before leaving Spain, I was able to gather
most of the information and consult with Spanish leaders before
beginning the actual work.

The libraries of Fuller Theological Seminary, the University of California at Los Angeles, and the public library of
Glendale, California were especially useful. Also the various
courses taken during my studies at the School of World Mission
have served to give me added insight in the areas of anthropology and theory that I trust have made this study of greater
value. Special appreciation has to be expressed to Dr. Ralph
Winter whose creative suggestions and careful guidance helped
to keep the goals clear before me. My fellow workers on the
field were very cooperative in sending materials as was a dear
friend, Gabino Fernández Campos. My wife, Anne, must also be
mentioned for her confidence in me beyond the call of duty and
for typing the final manuscript. It is through the efforts of
many that this work has become a reality.

The lack of some information on my part has made it impossible to do justice to all the various groups laboring in Spain.
The rapid increase of missionaries and the expansion of the
churches during the past five years has made it all but impossible to follow them. An attempt is made to present all efforts
as significant to the more important whole, but some activities
will undoubtedly appear slighted and even may have been completely overlooked. This is to be lamented and should be understood to have been done unintentionally.

In cases where the source material is in Spanish, the
translation is mine unless otherwise indicated.

Figure 1

IMPORTANT DATES IN THE
HISTORY OF THE CHURCH IN SPAIN

A.D.	EVENT
64?	Paul visits Spain?
254	First persecution of Christians in Spain.
589	First persecution of the Jews by the Church and the State combined.
710	Invasion of Spain by the Moors.
718	Beginning of the *"Reconquista."*
1478	Papal Bull issued authorizing the Inquisition in Spain.
1492	Termination of the *"Reconquista."*
	Union of Church and State under the Catholic Kings - Isabel and Ferdinand.
1559	*Autos-de-fe* in Valladolid and Seville.
1781	Last victim of the Inquisition.
1886	Spanish Revolution (Religious toleration).
1931	Second Republic (Religious liberty).
1936-39	Spanish Civil War.
1939	Reestablishment of the union of Church and State.
1953	Concordat signed with the Vatican.
1962-65	Second Vatican Council in Rome.
1967	Law of Religious Liberty Passed.

1
THE PHENOMENON
OF PLURALISM

One of the phenomena of the past thirty years has been
the trend towards human society becoming increasingly pluralistic. This trend has by now become a worldwide phenomenon.
The retreat of Western colonialism and the rise of new nations
has brought to the fore a critical need for a new appreciation
of diversity. It has been found that two or more cultures can
dwell together amiably within the same society. Also, many
nations that have tried to suppress cultural groups in the past
have now reevaluated their programs and see the value of unity
that does not require uniformity. There is a greater acceptance of social differences within the same culture in many
areas of the world. It is even becoming acceptable to permit
philosophical pluralism among nations which have traditionally
resisted it. One example of this is Spain. Without enumer-
ating specific illustrations, and in order to stay within the
sphere of this study, I will not emphasize the cultural, social,
political, or even the philosophical elements of pluralism that
are present in Spain today. Our study is to be directed to the
phenomenon of religious pluralism.

Immediately following the Civil War in Spain and for the
next fifteen years, it would have been difficult to conceive of
religious pluralism as a possibility. Long years of isolation
had built strong walls of prejudice and those walls were not
to be brought down easily.

When faced with the three phenomena of a universally
transforming force in the modern world (Protestantism,
the French Revolution, and Marxism), Spain knew how
to play her part with the dignity required of her.
Against Luther, she juxtaposed Trent; against Napoleon,
the War of Independence; and against Karl Marx, the
War of Liberation (the Crusade*). Spain is the only
nation that has shed her blood to check the heresy
of Protestantism, the dissolving spirit of the French
Revolution, and the demolishing thought of Marxist
socialism (Irizarry 1965:359).

Outwardly Spain has maintained the appearance of unity and
the ability to resist any intruding ideological force. This
chapter seeks to explain the background from which the phenomenon of religious pluralism has recently emerged in Spain.

THE PLURALISTIC POSITION

The uniqueness of Spain has been proclaimed far and wide
for many years. Looked upon as the citadel of Roman Catholicism, Spain generated an attitude of being the one country in
the world designated as the defender of the true faith. The
famous historian Menéndez and Pelayo expressed this attitude
so well in the epilogue of his classic work *Historia de los
heterodoxos españoles.* "Spain, evangelist to half the universe;
Spain, the scourge of heretics, the light of Trent, the sword
of Rome, the cradle of Saint Ignatius; ... that is our great-
ness and our unity: we have no other."

Although there was the outward appearance of unity, in-
wardly there were reappearing turmoils. A portion of the
people were not content to live in isolation and began to speak
up. They encouraged closer ties with the rest of Europe and a
more liberal attitude politically and socially. One person of
this group was Dionisio Ridruejo, former Director General of
Information. In speaking of his country he says:

The Church has great influence over the majority of
the middle class and the rural people. Hence, civil
peace cannot be achieved in Spain unless the Church

---

*The Spanish Civil War of 1936-1939.

accepts the new situation and liberalizes her point
of view. The Church in Spain, and those she influences, must live in peaceful coexistence with those
whose political viewpoints are not necessarily of
catholic inspiration.

His recognition of the need for change did not cause him
to feel that there was much hope for it to become a reality as
he continued, saying:

But don't think there is any prospect of Protestant
plurality in Spain. The Spaniard tends to adhere to
his traditional religion, or to live in agnosticism
apart from religion. Frequently he evades decision
on this question. What I mean is, he lives without
religious practices, allowing the religious problems
to remain peripheral in his life, without breaking
with the Church, either formally or in conviction
(Ridruejo 1963:94).

This was the type of thinking that the Catholic Church has
encouraged in Spain. It has wanted the people to feel that
there could be no possibility of another religious point of
view. The position of the Catholic Church was based on three
premises. 1. Religious liberty would be detrimental to the
unity of the State. 2. The Catholic Church is the only true
church, and, therefore, no other has the right to exist. 3.
Religious liberty would encourage the Protestant in efforts to
proselyte. A sample of this style of thinking can be seen in
the following expression of the Metropolitan Conference of
Bishops in May 1948.

Freedom of worship for individuals is false, if it is
considered as the right of each person to practice the
religion that he chooses or deems proper. For the
faithful there should be no freedom of choice between
one church and another, since they have the sacred duty
which is easily recognized by its signs and marks of
unity, sanctity, Catholicity, and apostolicity ...
As it is necessary for the State to practice a religion,
it should be the one true faith, that which is easily
recognized as such, above all in Catholic countries,
where the signs of truth are all the more apparent.
Those who govern should practice and protect this

religion as it is their duty to consider the well
being of their fellow-citizens (Delpech 1956:31).

How this negative attitude of the Spanish hierarchy has
been largely overcome by the Protestants and changed is related
in the next chapter. Needless to say, the Protestants were not
content to be treated as second-class citizens in their own
country. It was their conviction that pluralism was not only
desirable, but necessary. Their concept of religious freedom
did not call for preferential treatment, only the right to
believe and worship as they saw fit. They looked upon religious
freedom as a divine right, a moral good, and the desire of the
nation as a whole. Hence the 1950's were years when petitions
were made to the government protesting the way in which the
Protestants were being treated. It took time for these pleas
to gain a hearing and some changes are still taking place, but
pluralism is now a reality. The path leading to pluralism has
not been an easy one for those involved, but it will be worth
the trip for everyone. First of all, we will look at pluralism
from the position of the Catholic Church.

CATHOLIC POWER

In Spain the Catholic Church has enjoyed a position of
power unparalleled in any other country of the world. From
time to time that power has been challenged, both from without
and from within, but to no avail. The Church is firmly established. Since the days of the Catholic Kings, Ferdinand and
Isabel, the Catholic Church has been the largest single influence in Spanish life. Children are taught in school that they
are Spanish and Catholic as though the two were inseparable.
No one would care to challenge the statement that Spain is a
Catholic country. So strong is the feeling that there is often
heard the expression that Spain is more Catholic than the Pope,
and it would appear to be true. One person has expressed the
spirit of the nation in these words:

In the historical drama of Spain, the individual ...
tended to absorb the nation, the nation then proceeded
to absorb the world. In its passion for universality
Spain absorbed the Church, the most universal reality
in existence. The result was the conversion of the
state itself into a church (Mackay 1933:19).

That Spain would be so strongly Catholic would seem to be in direct contradiction of the strongest characteristic of the Spaniard -- individualism. Dr. Orts González considered this adherence to the Catholic Church as:

> the enigma of the Iberian peoples. How can one explain that a people so given by nature to personal individualism, so adverse to rules, standards, and restrictions, should accept Romanism, a system based upon an external authority which claims to be infallible, and which brings with it, besides, an immense amount of dogma and spirit so strict and rigid that it leaves scarcely any chance for the expression of individual life (García & Grubb 1933:13)?

Perhaps the real reason for their acceptance of Catholicism is best expressed in the words of the writer Díaz-Plaja when he says, "The Spaniard defends the catholic religion because it is his, and being his, it has to be perfect" (1969:53).

Spain has been the country that through the years has continued to maintain the Catholic Church at home and abroad with its wealth and blood. During the 16th century for example, she was responsible for sending out thousands of missionaries. Through the years the Church continued to increase in personnel and property. By the end of the 18th century, the physical presence of the Church was already quite substantial in Spain.

> In 1788 Spain had some 2,000 convents and monasteries for men and over 1,000 for women, containing 68,000 monks and 33,000 nuns. There were moreover 88,000 secular clergy and several thousand other religious officers. This made a total of close to 200,000 ecclesiastics in a population of 10,000,000.
> (Herr 1969:29).

More important than this, however, and more directly related to the well-being of the common people, was the amount of land controlled by the Church. "The census of 1797 showed 2,592 cities, towns, and villages under the jurisdiction of the Church (señorío eclesiástico) exclusive of Aragon" (Herr 1969:89). This did not give the ownership of the land to the Church, only its control. This combined with what the Church owned outright, gave it more land than was controlled by the State.

In recent years the Church has not been able to motivate such a large number of clergy as it has in past years, but it has gained in property and political power. One of the reasons for this unusual accumulation of power has been because of the special place of privilege granted to the Church by the Spanish government. In 1953 Spain became one of the few countries in the world to sign a Concordat with the Vatican. In that Concordat are spelled out in detail the various obligations of the State to the Church. The fact that Spain sought a Concordat in the first place is a very unusual bit of history and has been a bone of contention ever since. The amazing thing is that the only concession that Spain seemed to gain from the Vatican was one that she already had; namely, the right to nominate Bishops. Franco had already received the "privilege of presentation" which the Spanish kings had enjoyed for over four centuries and which had been reinforced in the Concordat of 1851. The real reason for entering into the Concordat seems to be more in line with bolstering Spain's sagging image worldwide. Much hard bargaining was carried on and in the end the only concession to Spain, out of the 36 provisions, seems to be that of nominating Bishops. This, of course, was the main plum and for it Spain paid dearly. (See appendix A for the main provisions of the Concordat.)

One of the more political controversies of the agreement was concerned with Article 34.

The association of Spanish Catholic Action shall freely exercise their apostolate under the immediate supervision of the ecclesiastical hierarchy; as to other kinds of activities, they shall conform to the general legislation of the State.

This provision gave away the Falange labor union monopoly and, in fact, gave the Spanish hierarchy the right to organize Spanish workers for political action. It also means that a man can be deprived of his livelihood if he does not conform to the church's demands (Fernsworth 1954:637).

Special privileges are granted to the priests, such as the exemption from military service and an exemption from appearance in civil courts without authorization from the Vatican.

In addition, the Church receives subsidies, tax exemptions, and
its construction costs at the expense of the State. In 1972
the daily Madrid paper *Ya* reported that in 1971 the expense of
the Church cost Spain almost nine and a half million dollars
(*Ya*, 6 January 1972). This figure, which represents a large
sum of money in Spain, may not even be close to the actual cost.
In 1964 the Spanish Government "awarded the church 1,026,978,967
pesetas (over seventeen million dollars) which figures, according
to *El Español*, would soon be raised by vote of the law of
July 28, 1963" (Irizarry 1966:328). It is doubtful that the
costs have decreased over the years.

This emphasis on power and property has made the Church
unpopular with the common people. Several times in Spanish
history the people have turned on the Church with bitter fury.
In the days of the Republic (1931-1935) the Church suffered
dearly. It is also reported that during the Civil War (1936-
1939) that 6,832 priests and nuns were put to death and most of
the churches and convents were burned to the ground (Morena
1961:762). It may be one of the ironies of history that the
most Catholic country of the world has also been the cause of
the deaths of more priests and nuns than any other.

Foreign observers have often mistaken this disenchantment
with the clergy and the whole system as a sign of an antireligious spirit. Nothing could be farther from the truth.
There may be widespread discontent with the Church, but the
Spanish are very religious people. One of the paradoxes of the
Spanish people is their ability to denounce the Church with
heated fervency, stay away from its services with absolute con-
sistency, and yet be ready to die for it passionately. This
seems to be a part of the Spanish character that has passed
through the generations from the days when

> Hunted and dispossessed, they grew steeled to adver-
> sity. Held together for survival, they developed
> their clannishness and their fear of outsiders. Seeing
> their churches razed and replaced by heathen mosques,
> they blazed with religious zeal (Miller 1963:18-19).

Although it can normally be assumed that every Spaniard is
a Catholic, it would certainly be wrong to assume that every
Spaniard is an active follower of his faith. As mentioned, there
is an amazing capacity on the part of the Spaniard to defend the

Church, but not to enter it. This needs to be understood if
one is to explain a good deal of what happens in Spain. There
is a popular story that explains this quite well. A visiting
protestant tourist was having his shoes shined by a young lad
when a priest passed by. The boy immediately began to casti-
gate the Church vociferously, much to the amusement and amaze-
ment of his client. This prompted the tourist to speak to the
lad concerning his faith with the idea of converting him. He
was cut short as the boy responded that if he couldn't believe
his own religion, which was the true one, how could he believe
that of the foreigner?

That there are many in Spain today that do not practice
any religion is undeniable. They are members of the Church,
but do not attend. Nor do they make any special pretence of
being "religious" except at special occasions. This has always
been true in Spain. Even Philip II is reported to have said
that he would gladly give up all the treasures of the Indies
for the conversion of one soul (Bustos 1934:120). He found
that the zeal and ardor for one's faith cannot be passed on to
one's children. His own son, Carlos, is reported to have become
a protestant. This was the cause of much consternation to his
father who had sworn to rid his kingdom of the heretics. When
Carlos died rather mysteriously on July 24, 1568, the evidence
indicated that if Philip did not order his death, he at least
permitted it (Castro 1851:373).

In more recent years the religious fervor of the people
has been the concern of the Catholic Church rather than the king,
but it still lags. When Cardinal Goma was Archbishop of Toledo,
his concern for the decay of ardor for the faith was expressed
in these words:

> We do not need to affirm that Catholicism within Spain
> has been in a state of decadence for a long time ...
> It is necessary to wipe out above all the absurd igno-
> rance of religion found in our country. I call it
> absurd because no country can afford to be as ignorant
> of Christ and religion as we are (Lord 1940:604-5).

His observations would seem to have been based upon solid facts
as the findings of Father Francisco Peiró revealed in his study
El problema religioso-social de España. He found that:

By 1931 only 5 per cent of the villages of New
Castile and Central Spain attended mass or carried
out the Easter obligations. In Andalucia the attendance of men was one per cent and in many villages
the priest said mass alone. The position in Madrid
was no better and in the parish of San Ramón in the
quarter of Vallecas, out of a population of 80,000
parishioners, only 3 1/2 per cent (excluding the
children of the convent schools) attended mass:
25 per cent of the children born were not baptized.
Of those educated in convent schools, 90 per cent
did not confess or hear mass after leaving school.
In other places the situation was worse (Breman 1962:
53).

The situation does not seem to have improved much if a
more recent survey conducted among 15,491 workers is indicative
of the rest of Spain. Of these workers it was found that 41.3
per cent declared themselves to be antireligious while 54.7 per
cent did not have any concern about religion. A full 86.1 per
cent stated that they were Catholics of the minimum obligations
(El Ciervo 1958:8). This means that they were baptized as
infants, were married by a priest, and when they die, will be
buried as a Catholic. The waning interest has not escaped the
notice of the Catholic authorities. A good many articles have
been devoted to this problem as well as a few books, trying to
arouse concern on the part of the priests and people.

Some of the Spaniards are more demonstrative in their disenchantment with the Church. The same report mentioned above
found that 89.6 per cent of the workers were anticlerical.
That a strong anticlerical feeling was common among the common
people of Spain was no secret, but its increase in recent years
has caused alarm among the hierarchy.

Even convinced catholics complain of the opulance,
worldliness, and 'commercialism' of the Church, and
the priests joke bitterly about the real-estate deals
and business methods of the powerful religious orders,
but the chief cause of the anticlericalism is the
Church's close association with the regime - one of
the few regimes on earth to have qualified for a papal
blessing (Alan 1962:235).

The result has been a definite bid to win back the working
class. An equivalent of a christian labor union called HOAC
and its younger counterpart JOC have been formed. These are
authorized by the catholic hierarchy and are leftist oriented.
Both groups have been permitted to associate themselves with
the problems of the workers and to cooperate with the left-wing
opposition. The idea is to form a Catholic trade union with
enough power to form a Christian Democrat Party on the French-
German-Italian model. The government is aware of the reformist
ambitions of Catholic Action (HOAC), and is trying to work out
a deal with the hierarchy to get control of the organization.
In order to do this, Franco is said to be willing to give up
his authority to name bishops in the Church.

Catholic Action, which had over 200,000 members in 1966,
has been instrumental in pointing out the fact that the unity
of the Church is not as strong as it used to be. A sort of
generation gap has developed. The 82 Spanish bishops average
65 years of age and are the stalwart defenders of the status quo.

All owe their appointment to Franco, and most are old
enough to still think of him primarily as the saviour
whose crusade spared the church from the terrors of
Communism. By contrast, most of Catholicism's influ-
encial lay leaders, and almost half of the 34,500
priests, are under 40. Many of the priests are of
working class origin, and feel strongly that the church
has lost touch with the masses (Time 1966:65).

Seeking to relate to the people more, the younger priests have
become the champions of the workers' social problems. Insti-
gating strikes and serving as "worker priests", they have continued to embarrass the hierarchy and the government. In 1966,
Catholic Action approved a resolution calling for the separation
of Church and State. The bishops promptly labeled the statement
as being too political in its intent and then banned all future
meetings of the organization (Time 1966:65). The group has
continued to function and another confrontation came in the
meeting of the Church Assembly in Septermber 1971. It was the
first time that bishops and priests met on an equal basis, and
a dramatic resolution was passed apologizing for the Church's
role in the Spanish Civil War. They also urged the breaking
of the Church-Government ties. A poll revealed that 55 per cent
of the priests were in favor of the separation of Church and

State. (U.S. News and World Report 1972:66).

Recent activities of the priests have done little to dispel the anticlerical attitude of the people. In early January 1971, there began to appear an unusually large number of articles in the newspapers of Spain in reference to the subject. Most of them expressed displeasure in the increased use of the sermon for the propagation of political and marxist propaganda. The government is also concerned about the political overtones of many of the church's activities and has warned that there should be more concern for the spiritual, not the political. In his state of the union speech on December 30, 1971, Franco said:

> The Catholic Church and the State constitute two
> powerful, vital forces which coincide in the pur-
> pose of bringing about the perfection of man and
> his spiritual and material wellbeing. Their ends
> cannot contradict each other, because it would
> produce a lamentable social crisis ... But what
> the State cannot do is to cross its arms before
> the determined attitudes of some ecclesiastics
> (*Ya* 31 December 1971:6).

In recent years the Concordat with the Vatican has once again become a point of contention. On the 29th of April 1968, Pope Paul VI sent a letter to Franco asking the Chief of State to renounce his privilege of nominating bishops. Franco's answer on the 12th of June made it clear that there would be no change on the part of Spain without a revision of other points on the part of the Vatican. He also referred to the consideration of the Spanish government of public opinion in the country (Monroy 1971:5). The discussion revolves around whether there will be a radical revision of the Concordat or its total abolition. To abolish the Concordat would certainly be more to Spain's benefit financially than it would be to the Vatican. A poll conducted by the magazine *Vida Nueva* among 5,600 persons, found that 61 per cent were for the complete abolishment of the Concordat, 31 per cent were in favor of making radical changes, and only 5 per cent asked that there be a revision of minor details (February 13, 1971).

In January 1973, a meeting of 83 churchmen voted by a large margin (59 for, 20 against, and 4 abstaining) for a loosening of the centuries old ties between the Church and State. The

text of the forty-eight page policy statement has not at this
time been released because of its presentation to the Vatican
and "high" government officials, but is reported to ask for:
1. An end to the government's share in nominating biships.
2. The withdrawal of members of the hierarchy from government
posts. 3. An end to the special legal privileges enjoyed by
priests. 4. The right of the "prophetic denunciation" of
social, political, and economic wrongs. 5. The continued
state support (financial) of schools, hospitals, and other
social service institutions operated by the church (Christianity
Today 1973:49-50). What will finally emerge from all of this
is a bit difficult to say right now, but it is evident that
both parties are dissatisfied with the situation that exists.

In spite of the internal strife and the controversy sur-
rounding the Church, its position is strong. Most of the newspapers and many of the magazines published in Spain are organs
of the Church. The educational system and most of the radio
and television programming is under control of the Church, and
films have to pass the Church censor before being shown. Thus,
nothing is read, seen, or heard without having passed the
censorship of the Church. Its influence is tremendous in every
area of life.

PROTESTANT PRESENCE

When confronted with the problem of the Protestants in
Spain, the usual response of government officials and Catholic
authorities was that of bewilderment. Considered as an insig-
nificant number, they were for some time not taken seriously.
After all, the Moslems and Jews, two other minority groups,
were not complaining about the treatment they received. Why
should the Protestants? This fact was used by the Spanish
authorities as justification for their intolerance for some
time. Several Catholic writers, in discussing the Protestant
situation, asked scornfully, "Would you be interested in
religious freedom for Eskimos in Panama" (Garrison 1950:1262)?

Numerically the Protestants have been a rather small group
in comparison with the population. According to the National
Catholic Almanac of the United States for 1961, the population
of Spain was 29,814,070. Of this number, 29,703,871 or 99.7
per cent of the population was Catholic. At the same time, a
most generous estimate of the Protestant community would have

been somewhere around 25,000. Not a particularly impressive
number unless you take into consideration the conditions under
which the Protestants were living in Spain.

It has become common practice to say that Protestantism is
a foreign import and not Spanish. Fernando Castiella, former
Foreign Minister for Spain, stated that "No true Protestant
tradition exists in Spain" (1964:190). Apparently he acquired
his information from the 138 page booklet published by the
Diplomatic Information Office of the Spanish Ministry of Foreign
Affairs in 1950. The booklet entitled *The Protestant Church in
Spain: Six Reports on an Anti-Spanish Campaign of Defamation*
was an effort to ease the pressure on Spain. Sr. Castiella
claims that Protestantism was the 19th century import at the
hand of "hawkers", referring to the activities of George Barrows
of the British and Foreign Bible Society. He cites only the
Spanish scholar, Luis Usoz y Río (1848-65) as being involved in
the beginning. Otherwise it was entirely in the hands of
foreigners.

While this would appear to be a valid judgment based on the
situation as it looked in the 19th century, it overlooks a good
bit of Spanish history. It is especially deceptive when one
considers the fact that the Inquisition had committed Spain to
"religious unity" by force for over three hundred years. John
David Lodge, former United States Ambassador to Spain, would
seem to support the opinion of Castiella when he says:

Spain was never exposed to the Protestant Reformation,
surely one of the most significant unheavals of modern
history. Indeed, Spain was the source, the center, and
the motive power of the Counter Reformation (Thomas1962:
7).

History would seem to support the opinion that the Reformation came at a most unfortunate time for the Protestants of
Spain. Had Luther delayed only a few months, Spain might well
have been the one to break with Rome. A movement had already
been under way for some time which was very similar to Lutheran-
ism in its ideals. Already a reform among the regular clergy
had been carried out by Cardinal Ximenez and there was a desire
for the Spanish clergy to be allowed to marry. There also
existed a dislike for the Italians and wholesale dissapproval
of the corruption of the Papacy. After the Spanish army sacked

Rome in 1527, there was a strong movement in Spain that considered taking away the temporal powers of the Pope. In addition to all this, the ideas of Erasmus had taken root all through Spain. The catholic historian González de Illezcas, in his *Pontifical History* states that "if two or three more months had passed in remedying this harm, it would have been embraced by all of Spain" (Varetto 1959:232).

When speaking of the 16th century in Spain and the Protestant Movement, it is normal to mention only the two larger communities of Valladolid and Sevilla. Generally overlooked is the fact that in many of the villages of old León, Zamora, the dioses of Palencia, and throughout all of Castilla clear to Soria and Logroño, there were followers of the reformed ideas. This was also true in Navarra and New Castile, and especially the city of Toledo, as well as the southern provinces of Granada and Murcia (M'Crie 1950:137-42). It is also significant that Cipriano de Valera wrote in the preface of his version of the Bible (1612) that there was

> no city, village or place in Spain that did not have
> someone or several whom God in his infinite grace had
> not illumined with the light of his Gospel; and al-
> though the adversaries had done everything possible to
> put out that light, facing the loss of their goods, of
> life and the honor of many, nothing was gained because -
> they say - the more they are confronted, the more they
> are beaten, forced to wear penitential garments, put
> into stocks or jailed for life or burned, the more
> they multiply (Varetto 1959:232).

The Protestant movement was in no wise confined to the ignorant and lower class peasants, but included the nobility, hierarchy, and even some of the court of Charles V himself. Thus, if Protestantism was a 19th century import to Spain, it was only because the Church and State had so forcefully and effectively combined to rid Spain of it for three centuries. When the door was opened in the late 1800's, it may have been a George Barrow who first drew the attention, but it was men like Manuel Matamoros, Juan Bautista Cabrera, Cipriano Tornos, and many more Spaniards who worked in reestablishing the Protestant church in Spain.

While the Protestant Community in modern times has never

been very large in Spain, its exact size has been difficult to
determine because of various circumstances. Probably the most
complete work of determining the size and location of the Protestant churches was done by García and Grubb in 1933. Their
figures are the most accurate ever given on this subject. In
1933 they list 166 churches with a communicant membership of
6,259. The total community was listed at 21,900. To minister
to the needs of this community there were 48 ordained ministers,
94 evangelists, and 123 foreign missionaries (1933:94). Right
on the heels of this work came the Spanish Civil War and the
termination of the Protestant Church, for all practical purposes,
for some 15 to 20 years.

For the past ten years, both in Spain and around the world,
it has been common to say that there are now 30,000 Protestants
in Spain. This figure was used as the title of a book on the
Protestants published in 1965 by Carmen Irizarry. The basis
for using this number was the figures released by the Spanish
Evangelical Defense Commission on May 24, 1961. Those figures,
obviously given in round numbers, are as follows:

Spanish Evangelical Church.	3.800
Reformed Episcopal Church	1.000
Spanish Evangelical Baptist Union	5.400
Federation of Independent Evangelical Churches of Spain	3.100
Plymouth Brethren	6.000
Assemblies of God	3.500
Seventh-day Adventists.	5.200
Independents.	2.000
Total.	30.000

The most serious attempt at determining the exact size and
distribution of the Protestants in Spain since the Spanish
Civil War was that of Juan Estruch. His work entitled *Los
Protestantes Españoles* was originally presented as a thesis at
the University of Barcelona in June 1967 and published in January 1968. The value of his work lies mainly in the maps giving
the distribution of the various churches by province and the
more detailed report on the city of Barcelona. His figures on
the size of the Protestant Church in Spain are for the same year
as the Defense Commission's report (1961) and are:

	Min.	Max.
Spanish Evangelical Church.	2.544	3.062
Reformed Episcopal Church	558	697
Spanish Evangelical Baptist Union	3.472	4.060
Federation of Independent Evangelical Churches of Spain	1.006	1.163
Spanish Christian Mission	488	693
Plymouth Brethren	5.012	5.849
Assemblies of God	218	665
Various	517	665
Total Protestants	13.816	16.470

	Min.	Max.
Non-Catholics that are not Protestants.	2.307	2.934
Jews.	3.600	3.600
Total Non-Catholics	19.723	23.004

The non-Catholics, not counted as Evangelicals, are as follows:

	Min.	Max.
Seventh-day Adventists.	1.329	1.607
Jehovah's Witnesses	635	857*
Quakers	52	75
Baha'is (Oriental Society).	141	195
Greek Orthodox.	150	200
Jews.	3.600	3.600
Total	5.907	6.534

(Estruch 1968:39).

*The figures given for the Jehovah's Witnesses are estimates on the part of Estruch as he tells in a footnote. He assumes that the group is much larger than the figure he gives.

Figure 2
SIZE OF THE EVANGELICAL GROUPS IN 1961

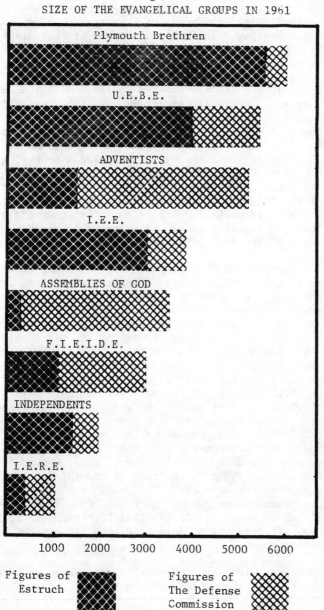

A comparison of the figures of the Spanish Evangelical
Defense Commission and those of Estruch reveal some of the
problem encountered in doing a study of this type. By including
the Seventh-Day Adventists* in the total number of Protestants,
as given by Estruch, we come up with just over half as many
Protestants as listed on the Defense Commission's report. Sr.
Estruch estimates that the true figure would be about 20,000
Protestants in 1961, but still not up to the 30,000 listed by
the Defense Commission. The difference may well be that Estruch
is counting actual church members (*miembros comulgantes*) while
the Defense Commission is counting the total community (*miembros
congregantes*). In Spain it is not uncommon for people to attend
a Protestant Church for some time before becoming a member, if
ever. Some churches include these sympathizers when reporting
the size of their church, others do not. The *World Christian
Handbook* for 1968 lists the actual membership in 1967 as 19,218
and the total community at 42,678. I believe that they are a
bit low and that the actual size of the Protestant Church in
Spain in 1961 was closer to 20,000 than 30,000.

Trying to decide how much the church had grown during the
ten years from 1961 to 1970, I sent out a questionnaire to all
of the churches in Spain in the spring of 1971. The results
were not very satisfactory. I did not receive a large enough
response to give an accurate figure. In past years the churches
have not been accustomed to keeping records of the membership.
Of those that do keep these records, I found that the majority
were not anxious to share the information with others. Fortunately, I have had the cooperation of some of the church leaders,
especially the F.I.E.I.D.E., and can make a reasonable estimate
of the size of the Protestant Church in Spain. I would estimate
that the present actual church membership of the Protestants in
Spain is around 30,000. This would not indicate any unusual
growth. I base my estimate on the fact that normal biological
growth (25 per cent per decade) would account for 5,000 additional church members. The previous rate of growth, if continued, would account for another 3,000. As I have already
mentioned, this is an estimate on my part. I trust that in the
future it will not be such a difficult task to obtain statistics
on the churches. The new Law of Religious Liberty requires all

---

*The Seventh-Day Adventists are not usually considered as Evan-
gelicals by the rest of the Protestants in Spain.

churches that are registered to keep records on their membership and it would not be difficult for a report to be sent to
the Defense Commission for reference. This would be useful in
many ways.

One indication of the way in which the Protestant Church
is growing is the number of congregations. In 1933 there were
166 churches. At the end of the civil war in 1939, only about
five of these churches remained open. By 1961, there were 175
churches and 151 other groups in formative stages. In 1971,
the number had increased to 285 churches and 132 groups in
formation. (See Figure 1L)

There are three types of Protestant groups recognized
under Spanish Law. First is the registered church. Second is
a section of a registered church that meets in another place,
(Sección local) and the third is a place authorized as a site
for holding meetings (lugar de cultos). The last two are what
would normally be considered as mission points and the distinction between them in Spain is a technical one and it is
not necessary to elaborate on it here. The Protestant situation
as summed up in the report of the Evangelical Defense Commission
in 1971 was 417 churches or places of worship, and 363 pastors
and workers. Of the 417 places of worship, 311 are recognized
by the government. The breakdown is as follows:

- -

Name[1]	Places of worship	Legalized	Ministers
Brethren (Plymouth)	95	93	120
Southern Baptist	58	22	60
Spanish Evangelical Church	45	2	29
Federation of Independent Evangelical Churches of Spain	40	40	32
Assemblies of God	35	35	30
Pentecostal Evangelical Church	23	23	10
Gypsy Evangelical Movement	30	30	23
Reformed Episcopal Church	15	15	14
Darby Communities	15	--	--
Church of Christ	12	12	12
Church of God in Spain	10	10	2
Independent Baptist Communion	10	10	2
Churches of the New Testament	6	4	4
Spanish Evangelical Baptist Gr.	5	5	1

- -

Name[1]	Places of worship	Legalized	Ministers
Community of Pentecostal Evangelical Churches	5	5	3
Quakers	5	–	–
Pentecostal Assemblies of Spain	3	3	2
Jesus Only Church			
Apostolic Church of Spain	2	2	1

[1]Placed in order according to the number of churches.

Organization "Not Evangelical" but recognized by the Law
of Religious Liberty

	Places of worship	Legalized	Ministers
Association of Christian Churches of Seventh-Day Adventist	35	35	50
Adventist Church of the Reformed Movement	5	5	8
Adventist Church	4	4	6
Mormans	11	11	30
Christian Science	3	3	3
Baha'is (Spiritual Assembly)	15	15	15
Jehovah's Witnesses	80	80	Unknown

(*Portavoz* 1972:20)

From this list of denominations or organized associations of churches it is evident that there has been an increase in such groups during the past 10 years. In the list for 1961, there were only 8 groups listed, while now some 26 are recognized by the government. (Not all of them are Evangelical.)

The geographical distribution of the churches is important in understanding the Protestant situation in Spain. It follows the population distribution to a large degree and gives some idea of where Protestants are more readily received. The following map is compiled on an area basis and gives the distribution of the churches and groups for 1971. For a complete list by province, see Appendix B.

Figure 3

DISTRIBUTION OF PROTESTANT CHURCHES

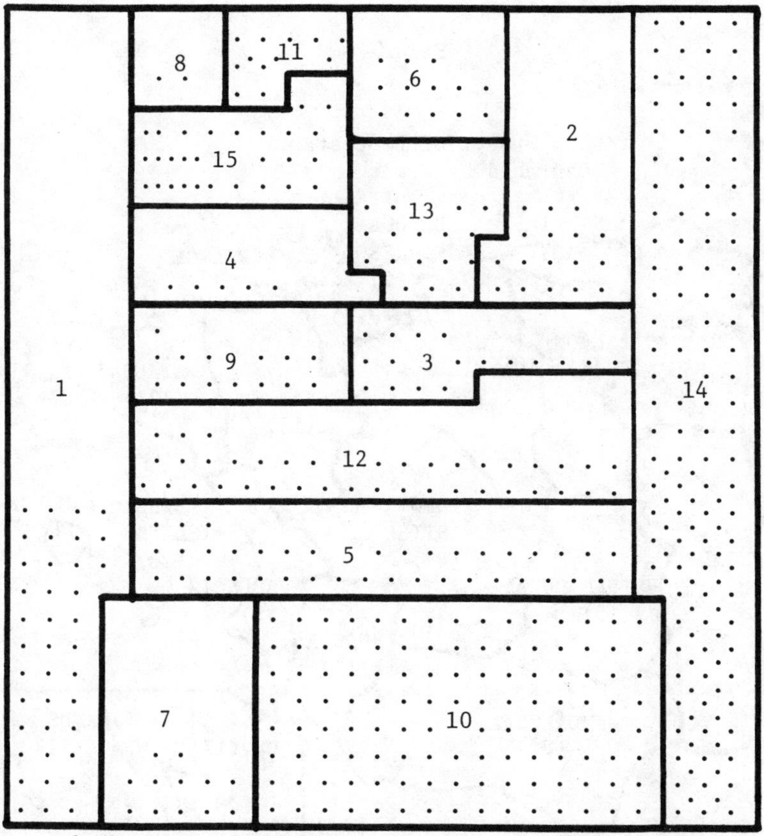

. = 1 Church   The entire square equals the population
                   of Spain - 33,000,000 1971
        Areas   Each small square = 55,000 people

1. New Castile   6. Asturias   11. Balearic Islands
2. Old Castile   7. Basque Provinces 12. Valencia
3. León   8. Navarra   13. Murcia
4. Extremadura   9. Aragón   14. Andalusia
5. Galicia   10. Catalonia   15. Canary Islands

Figure 4

The Number of Protestant
Churches by Areas - 1971

2

THE PATH TO PLURALISM

The impact of the Second Vatican Council on the Roman Catholic world has been dynamic. The small ripples that were begun
by the tossing of the ecumenical pebble into the sea of Catholicism have resulted in giant waves on many a distant shore.
Spain feared that the result would be more like a tidal wave.
The impact has been felt in Spain to a certain extent, but not
as favorably as the Protestants had hoped nor as unfavorably
as the Catholic Church had feared. This chapter deals with
three major factors in bringing about a pluralistic position in
the country of Spain. The religious pressures of the Second
Vatican Council and other ecumenical decisions, the strong world
opinion that does not permit any country to remain totally to
itself, and the political and economic pressure that force com-
promises have all influenced Spain in recent years. Since all
of these factors are so intertwined and too difficult to separate
for our purposes, the material is presented in chronological
order.

FROM THE CIVIL WAR
UNTIL THE SECOND VATICAL COUNCIL

One of the most unfortunate results of the Spanish Civil
War was the association of the Protestants with Communists.
When the war began in 1936, the Evangelicals of Spain united
with the Republican side, feeling it to be the lesser of two
evils and their only hope of continuing to exist in Spain. This
was the recognized government of Spain at the time, but it

received very little aid from the French, English, or American
governments in its time of need. It is claimed that these
countries were kept from aiding Spain because of pressures on
the part of the Catholic Church. The Nationalists were receiving
a substantial amount of aid from "neutral" Italy. With their
backs to the wall, the Republicans looked for help wherever they
could get it. It was to come mainly from Russia. The support
of some 240 planes, 700 cannons, 750 tanks, 29,000 tons of ammu-
nition, and nearly 1,000 "volunteer" specialists and advisors
(Goldston 1966:75) only helped prolong the fight. It was through
this turn of events that the Protestants of Spain became associated with the Communists in the minds of the Nationalists. This
has been a definite hindrance to the advancement of the Protestants in Spain.

THE PROTESTANTS AND THE STATE

The war ended in 1939 with the victory of the Nationalists
under the leadership of General Francisco Franco. The Roman
Catholic Church was immediately reestablished as the State Church.
Toward the end of the war Franco was urged to declare himself in
favor of freedom of worship after the war. He did go as far as
to send a letter to his envoy in England, the Duke of Alba, which
was published in The Times of London saying that "freedom would
be granted to all denominations" (Matthews 1957:177). After the
war, nothing came of this promise. In fact, the opposite occurred. It may be that Article 6 of the _Fuero de los Españoles_
(Charter of the Spanish People) which came into being in July
1945 was an effort to fulfill this promise. The article was the
fundamental legal statute regarding religious practice until
1967 and reads as follows:

> The profession and practice of the Catholic religion,
> which is that of the Spanish State, shall enjoy offi-
> cial protection. No one shall be disturbed because
> of his religious beliefs or the private practice of
> his worship. No outward ceremonies or demonstrations
> other than those of the Catholic religion shall be
> permitted.

The reestablishment of the Roman Catholic Church as the
State Church ushered in the most difficult years of recent times
for the Protestants of Spain. Articles appeared in the papers
calling Protestants evil Spaniards and on the radio influential

people expressed great displeasure that they should even be
allowed to exist. They were hard years.

> Life had become very difficult for the Evangelicals.
> Getting married, treatment in hospitals, admission
> to schools, military service, friendship, getting
> employment, and there were even difficulties over
> burials. All these situations were fraught with
> much hardship and frustration (Anonymous 1969:6).

The Civil War of 1936-39 had, for all practical purposes,
halted the progress of the Protestant Church and had caused it
great losses. Although there was not the severe persecution
of earlier centuries, there was less freedom than at any time
since 1868. In most areas the churches were completely closed.
Many of the pastors had been killed, were in exile, or imprisoned.
Many of the people did continue to meet secretely in homes, but
always in danger of apprehension by the authorities. Some were
arrested, fined, and imprisoned for this; but they continued on
in spite of the danger. It is largely because of the determina-
tion of these faithful few that the Protestants have freedom
in Spain today.

Because the Catholic Church has always been so involved in
political issues, it has assumed that the Protestant Church was
too. It is completely foreign to the Spanish Catholic mind
that Protestants as individuals can and do have interests in
politics, but that the Protestant churches as organizations do
not. This lack of making distinctions between the individual
and the group has continually been detrimental to the Protestant
Church in Spain.

The Confidential Letter of November 12, 1945

The government's attitude towards the Protestants since
the Civil War has come largely from the Catholic Church. Little
attention was given to the situation of the Protestants in Spain
by the rest of the world at this time because of World War II.
After the war ended, the world did begin to note the things that
were happening in Spain. In the late 40's there was a bit of
a relaxing attitude toward the Protestants which caused the
Catholic Church some alarm. It was decided that the wording of
Article 6 of the *Fuero* was too ambiguous, especially in respect
to "private practice of his worship" and on November 12, 1945,
a confidential letter of surprising liberality was sent to the

Civil Governors of the provinces by the Minister of Interior.
The letter reads:

Your Excellency:
At the outset of the glorious National Movement* it
was necessary to suspend worship and therefore to close
down the chapels of certain non-Catholic confessions in
Spanish territory, owing on the one hand to the hos-
tility evinced towards the new State by some rectors
of these chapels or persons in charge of them, and on
the other to the danger they might involve to the
indispensable spiritual unity of Spaniards. The causes
for this measure having disappeared, and for the complete restoration of a juridical situation normal in
our country, the restoration of this dissident worship
has been authorized by the *Fuero* (Charter), which, in
announcing individual guarantees, lays down in its
Article 6, that 'no one shall be molested for his
religious beliefs or the private practice of his worship,' stating moreover that 'no outward manifestations or ceremonies other than those of the Catholic
religion shall be permitted.' Accordingly, from now
on, what is ordered by the statute must be observed.
Within the limits laid down, the above-mentioned confessions can thus enjoy the tolerance provided.
By virtue of these provisions, this Ministry, after
deliberation by the Cabinet, states as follows:
(1) The confessions dissident from the Catholic
Religion may practice their private worship throughout
the country, provided that services are always held
inside their respective places of worship, and there
is no manifestation or demonstration on the public
thoroughfare.
The representatives of the said confessions or the
persons in charge of this worship may likewise organize religious ceremonies on condition that they do
not turn them to, or associate them with other ends,
whether political, propaganda associations of pro-
hibited kinds, or otherwise than exclusively devotion-
al or more broadly, having to do with the cult.
(2) Authorization to open such places of worship
must be applied for in each case to the Civil Governor

*The Civil War of 1936-39.

of the province in which they are situated; such
Governor, after due report, may grant leave according
to the present rules. He must inform this Ministry
thereof. The authorization must also be made known
to those who apply for it.

(3) Civil Governors shall protest the practice of
the worship they authorize and must not interfere
with the carrying out of the services by which the
said cults fulfill their spiritual duties, nor in
the private acts of these confessions (Delpech 1955:
54-5).

The letter clarified what was meant by "private worship" to
some extent and implies that worship was to be a private act.
The letter also refers to all non-Catholic faiths as "cults."

The Decree of February 23, 1948

By 1948 the reaction of the leaders of the Catholic Church
was so strong for a more restrictive interpretation of Article
6 of the *Fuero* that the Ministry of the Interior issued a very
restrictive decree. Dated February 23, 1948, it read:

Under the cloak of the toleration established by
Article 6 of the *Fuero*, abuses have been committed
and the protests of the Church authorities and the
people against the infringements on this connection
are numerous.

In addition, before our crusade, it even happened
that the Protestant churches concealed Masonic centers
of conspirators against the public order.

Therefore, it must be determined, clearly and unequiv-
ocally, what are the differences between (a) the private
exercise of worship of the dissident denominations and
the proper respect for their conscience, and (b) abuses
and infringements, attempted under the cloak of toleration. The test of the law, both in word and in spirit,
admits only one interpretation and application:

(1) The exercise of private worship of non-Catholic
religions is recognized.

(2) By 'private worship' is meant strictly personal
worship, or services inside the building consecrated
to the denomination in question.

(3) This worship may in no case be manifested out-

wardly or publically, in the first place, because
it would no longer be private, which is the only form
allowed, and, in the second place, because no outward ceremonies or demonstrations are allowed, other
than those of the Catholic religion.
  (4) In consequence, all propaganda or proselytism
for non-Catholic religions is illicit, whatever the
methods used, as for instance, the founding of schools
for teaching; the distribution of gifts, supposedly
with charitable intent; the operation of recreational
centers, summer camps, etc.; for these would obviously
be outward ceremonies or demonstrations, which are
not allowed.

It is highly significant that the first public disclosure of
this decree was not made for two years. It came to light in
the reply of the Chief of the Civil Cabinet of the Chief of
State, dated March 16, 1950 to a petition addressed to Generalisimo Franco by some Protestant leaders.

The 1950 Protestant Petition

  The petition which had been sent to the Chief of State,
outlined the difficulties of the Protestant community and urged
that "measures be taken in regard to the laws upon which our
situation depends, and that they be applied in the same manner
throughout the nation." The petition listed sixteen points in
all and the following are specific points mentioned as being
especially needed:

  (1) Precise measures concerning the reopening and
  inauguration of places specifically designated for
  Protestant whorship, so as to leave no room for doubt
  in the minds of local authorities.
  (2) Guarantees that our services may be held without hindrance or trouble.
  (3) Authorization to print Bibles, hymnbooks, and
  also other works of meditation and theology, as is
  done by other denominations now predominant among
  Christian churches: these books to be reserved for
  the exclusive use of our churches.
  (4) Authorization to hold our services in private
  homes whenever a better spot cannot be found, upon
  notifying the authorities in advance.

(5) The reopening and the founding of schools for Protestant families.

(6) Respect for the conscience of pupils and students who frequent public or private schools.

(7) Guarantees to enable the obtaining of a civil marriage when it is requested by the members of the churches.

(8) The right for Spanish Protestants to make application for social-welfare assistance without getting drawn into expressed or implied requirements that would be impossible or at least very difficult for them to accept.

(9) Exemption from Catholic religious observances for Protestants under military or penal jurisdiction as well as the right to receive the spiritual aid of their own pastors.

(10) The assurance of being able to bury our dead with a religious ceremony in civil cemeteries, or, if there is no such cemetery, an absolute guarantee that the place where they are buried will be guaranteed against danger of profanation (*Carta Circular* 1950:3-6).

The answer to the petition was signed by the Chief of the Civil Cabinet of the Chief of State. It stated only that "he referred the matter to the Minister of the Interior, who had given him as a reply, a copy of the circular sent to all provincial governors." This is the restrictive decree of 1948 mentioned previously.

The Spanish Evangelical Defense Commission

In 1951 the majority of the Spanish Protestant groups united in the formation of an organization to represent them before the government. Called the Spanish Evangelical Defense Commission, (presently the Evangelical Service of Legal Assistance), it became the agency unofficially recognized by the government for the representation of all Protestants and has done an outstanding job.

World Council of Churches Declaration of 1948

While there was pressure being applied by the Protestants within the country for greater liberty, world opinion was beginning to be felt also. The mood of the world was for religious liberty everywhere. The World Council of Churches at its

meeting in Amsterdam in 1948 had come out with a strong declaration on religious freedom which was to cause more pressure to
be applied to nonconformist nations. The four basic points to
come out of that Amsterdam meeting were:

1. Every person has the right to determine his own faith
    and creed.
2. Every person has the right to express his religious
    belief in worship, teaching and practice, and to pro-
    claim the implications of his belief for relation-
    ships in a social or political community.
3. Every person has the right to associate with others
    and to organize with them for religious purposes.
4. Every religious organization, formed or maintained by
    action in accordance with the rights of the individual
    persons, has the right to determine its policies and
    practices for the accomplishment of its chosen pur-
    poses (Carrillo de Albornoz 1963:157-8).

Possibly in partial response to the World Council of
Churches Declaration, at least one of Franco's Ministers was
becoming aware of the world mood as early as 1953. This was
Fernando María Castiella y Maíz who was Foreign Minister. He
took to heart the words of Pope Pius XII delivered at the Fifth
Convention of Italian Catholic Jurists in 1953. "It asked
Catholic statesmen to study the facts of the situation in which
he was involved, so as to determine whether in concrete instances,
tolerance can be 'justified in the interest of a higher and
more general good'" (Castiella 1964:189). To Castiella that
meant the Protestant situation in Spain.

In his position as Foreign Minister, Castiella was in contact with the diplomatic and political leaders of the world.
Feeling that much of the anti-Spanish feeling in the world was
due to the anti-Protestant attitude of Spain, Castiella set
himself to do something about the situation. It is largely the
result of his efforts, combined with those of José Cardona,
Secretary of the Spanish Evangelical Defense Commission, that
things moved as quickly toward religious freedom as they did.
Sr. Castiella was responsible for the government's compensating
the British and Foreign Bible Society for a police raid on its
headquarters in 1956, and he also blocked the efforts of a
Catholic group to close a Baptist Seminary in Barcelona.

Difficult Times All Around

The 1950's were the years when Spain began to end its ostracism from the rest of the world. The prestige of the country was at a low ebb when Franco negotiated two important agreements. The first was the Concordat with the Vatican, and the second was with the United States allowing military bases on Spanish soil. The text of the Concordat was kept secret for a month in order not to jeopardize negotiations with the United States. The Falange would certainly have tried to disrupt the bargaining had it known that Franco had given away their labor union monoply just a month previously (Fernsworth 1954:637-9).

During this same time period, the Catholic Church was continuing its fight to discredit the Protestants in Spain. On November 25, 1953, *Fe Católica* (a Jesuit organization) presented to Generalismo Franco, in a special audience, a detailed report entitled *"El Protestantismo en España."* It was a report of some 80 pages given only to high government officials. It was extremely detrimental to the Protestants. Unfortunately, the report was influential in determining the policy of the government in respect to the Protestants and it was not until the erroneous information of that report was disproved that progress began to be made towards religious liberty.

Under the strain of economic incompetence and corruption, Spain nearly went bankrupt in 1959. It narrowly averted such a catastrophe by securing loans from the United States and the Organization for European Economic Cooperation, along with advisors who arrived just in time. These circumstances forced Spain to adopt a stabilization plan and to change many of its policies in reference to foreign investments and trade. The success of that stabilization plan was fantastic and led to the economic development plan of the 1960's.

The Law of Religious Liberty Proposed

In 1961, developments began to take shape for Spain's move toward a pluralistic position. Sr. Castiella, the Foreign Minister, in a private audience with Pope John XXIII, presented a proposal which would give Protestants more freedom in Spain. Explaining that thousands of non-Catholics were visiting Spain each year, he asked, "Is it better for the people to spend their

Sundays cavorting on the beaches, or worshipping God in their
own way?" The Pope replied, "You are right, my son, leave the
draft with me" (Time 1963:35). During that same year, there
were some evidences of a relaxed attitude toward the Protestant
community. The Spanish government authorized the reopening of
the Baptist Church in Seville, which was one of six churches
closed by the police in 1958. The permission, which was granted
after studying the situation for some time, made it clear that
the government did not give a general acknowledgment that the
Evangelical Churches had the right to exist. It also warned
that the permission to operate was conditional upon the strict
observances of the "private nature of worship services" by the
members and church leaders. The church was also forbidden to
engage in any activities of proselytism.

Early in 1962 a notable decision was handed down by the
Spanish Supreme Court of Appeals upholding the right of a young
Evangelical couple to be married in a civil ceremony even
though they had been baptized as Catholics when infants. The
decision for Mario Garralon and Carmen Sánchez came only after
more than three years of appealing the case (Christian Century
1962:402).

The address of Don Antonio Garrigues, Spanish Ambassador to
the United States, to the National Press Club in Washington
stirred up great hopes among those interested in the Protestants'
situation in Spain. In speaking of a new status for non-Catholics
he said that he believed in "absolute freedom." He went on to
say, "I will tell you very frankly that I am a Catholic, but we
believe in liberty for Protestants as well." "I recognize,"
he continued, "that we in Spain have committed an error against
the Protestants. Nevertheless, I can assure you, that we are
trying to remedy the situation and give to the Spanish Protestants the status they desire," (as some reports said) or "The
status they deserve" (as others reported). The reason this
was of such importance was because up until that time, Spain
had given no indication publicly that a religious liberty law
was even under consideration. All considerations of this type
were secret and in Spain all reference to this remark was
deleted from the papers. Ambassador Garrigues issued a corrected
text which he sent to the Washington Post which dispelled the
hopes of the Protestants. He contended that he had said, "I
do recognize that we in Spain may have committed some errors
towards Protestants, but we will avoid in the future such mis-

understandings and will give to the Protestants the position
they have the right to have in Spain under Spanish laws." Since
there were few rights given under the laws at that time, the
Ambassador had retracted the basis for hope (<u>Christian Century</u>
1962:402).

The world press picked up the story and published it far
and wide. Four months later the <u>Catholic Herald</u> of London published four articles entitled "Spain in a Period of Transition."
In one of the articles the law concerning Protestants in Spain
was again mentioned as well as affirming that "Few things have
done more harm to Spain than her attitude towards the Protestant
minority" (Monroy 1967:45).

FROM THE SECOND VATICAN COUNCIL
TO THE PASSING OF THE LAW OF RELIGIOUS LIBERTY

The pressures from within the Catholic Church for a change
in Spain were only reinforcements of world opinion. It was
becoming more apparent that something would have to be done
and the Spanish Church would have to make some concessions. A
secret meeting of the Metropolitan Council, composed of fifteen
ranking prelates, including four Cardinals, met in Madrid in
early 1963 to discuss a religious liberty law. They approved,
in principle, Castiella's "Statute for Non-Catholic Religions."
The substance of the statute, while prohibiting proselyting,
allowed judicial recognition to the major Protestant churches
as religious groups. It also made allowance for Protestants
to run their own schools and seminaries, print and distribute
their own Bibles, and operate hospitals and cemeteries. It
even affirmed the right of Spanish Protestants to hold every
civil office except that of the Chief of State (<u>Time</u> 1963:35).
Their consideration of a law of religious liberty did not keep
the Spanish delegations from opposing the idea when it was
presented to the delegates in session at the Second Vatican
Council. Bishop Emile Joseph DeSmedt of Belgium opened general
debate on the subject on November 19, 1963. He pointed out that:

> Many non-Catholics harbor an aversion against the
> Church or at least suspect her of a kind of Machia-
> vellism because we seem to them to demand the free
> exercise of religion when Catholics are in a minority
> in any nation and at the same time refuse and deny the
> same religious liberty when Catholics are in the
> majority" (Küng, Congar & O'Hare 1964:237-8).

P. H. WELSHIMER MEMORIAL LIBRARY
MILLIGAN COLLEGE
MILLIGAN COLLEGE, TENN. 37682

The Spanish, Italian, and some of the Latin American delegates
fought back. Cardinal de Arriba y Castro of Spain opposed free
worship saying that it "will ruin the Catholic Church if it is
put in effect in those states where Catholicism is the leading
religion ... Only the Catholic Church has the right to preach
the Gospel" (Blanchard 1966:78).

The opposition of the Spanish Fathers to the declaration
of Vatican II brought instant criticism from around the world.
The proposal, however, received more backers as time passed and
by the end of the second session, it was clear that the majority
of the Council was in favor of making some kind of declaration
in favor of religious liberty. There was a wide gulf between
the delegates on the details of the proposal and it was returned
to a committee for changes. The political maneuverings behind
the scenes by the Spanish and Italian delegates caused delays
and almost succeeded in keeping the proposal from reaching the
floor on a vote. In the October 10, 1964 issue of *Ya*, a Madrid
daily, it was reported that the Pope had told one of the
Spanish Cardinals:

> Don't be afraid of religious liberty, I know full
> well that the circumstances in Spain are very special,
> and I will be with Spain. But the Spaniards should
> be with the Pope; they must not fear religious liberty.

Still it was only the direct intervention of the Pope that
brought the declaration onto the floor for a vote on the final
day of the Council. By a vote of 1,997 to 224 the Declaration
of Religious Liberty became the first formal declaration of its
kind by the Roman Catholic Church. The final phraseology of
the declaration apparently involved some compromise with the
dissenting delegates. Its interpretation can be adjusted somewhat to suit the desire of the interpreter, but it was strong
enough to put pressure on Spain to do something. There was
great expectation among the Protestants of Spain and there were
some improvements in the situation, but it was not until
February 26, 1968 that the New York Times reported, "The Catholic Church in Spain, once the last redoubt of medievalism, is
responding to the progressiveness of Pope John XXIII and Pope
Paul VI."

The Opposition Lessens

While the debates were being carried on in the chambers of

the II Vatican Council, there were some encouraging signs of
freedom taking place in Spain. In early 1963 ten more Evangelical churches were allowed to reopen. Also, the 131-year-
old British and Foreign Bible Society was allowed to resume
operations in Madrid. In March of the same year, Roger Schuty,
Prior of the Protestant Community of Taize in France, was
invited to participate in a "Week of Contemporary Thought" at
the Church of the Redeemer (Catholic) in Seville (Christian
Century 1963:1527).

On October 3, 1963, permission for a non-Catholic convention was granted to the Spanish Baptist Union. The permission
was granted by the Alicante provincial delegation of the
Ministry of Information and Tourism, with the consent of the
governor of the province. In the statement of permission, the
word "convention" was avoided and the meetings were referred to
as the XIV Synod of the Spanish Baptist Union. The granting of
such permission was significant because it showed a more positive approach to the Protestant situation. In the past, the
government had not denied the permission; they simply ignored
the request. Conventions had been held, but never with the
direct permission of the government (Christian Century 1963:
1927).

By November 1963, the Spanish government had given permission for the sale and distribution of nine Evangelical books.
In December it was announced that Immanuel Baptist Church in
Madrid would be permitted to post a notice of the times of service outside its chapel. Notices of this type had been barred
before on grounds that they violated the Spanish Constitution
which forbids any external religious manifestations by groups
other than the Roman Catholic Church (Commission 1963:15).
Although this was of importance, it did not have the impact
that it could have had since Immanuel Baptist Church is an
English-speaking church for American servicemen at the Air Force
Base outside of Madrid.

The evidence seemed to indicate that the effects of Pope
John XXIII's conciliatory attitude was beginning to have an
effect in Spain. Bishop Cantero Cuadrado stressed the need to
"proceed cautiously in such a delicate matter" as broader rights
for Protestants. Spain, he said, is "neither mentally nor
psychologically prepared for the exercise of religious liberty
to the extent regarded as normal and even indispensable in

other countries" (Newsweek 1963:78).

In spite of the encouraging signs of freedom, there were
still cases of persecution. In Barcelona José Grau and Salvador
Salvado were sentenced to a month and a day in prison for publishing an unauthorized religious book. The booklet was *El
Cristiano-ese desconocido* (Christian Century 1962:76). In 1963
six churches were refused permission to reopen, and fines
totaling about $480.00 were levied against the Evangelicals by
provincial officials for "holding meetings without authorization." Fortunately, the incidents of this type were becoming
fewer and, in general, the situation looked hopeful.

On February 15, 1964, it was reported that the Pope had
received for study the text of the proposed Spanish law to
grant more freedom to the Protestants. According to the report
in the London Sunday Telegraph, the bill was approved with minor
amendments by the Council of Twelve Spanish Archbishops. The
admittedly unofficial sources said that the draft included the
following provisions:

1. The State would recognize baptism and marriage certif-
   icates issued by Protestant clergymen after church
   ceremonies.
2. Protestant schools would be authorized after prior
   approval by the local bishop.
3. The right of Protestants to obtain commissions in
   the armed forces and to hold public office would be
   clarified.
4. Protestant congregations would be entitled to own
   property (American 1964:300).

The Law Revealed

It was obvious that Spain was considering a significant
move closer to genuine pluralism. Actually, the proposal had
been kept as a State secret for over three years while it
passed through various committees. Although there was only
speculation as to what would finally emerge, there was hope.
The proposal, up to this point, was far from conferring complete freedom to the Spanish Protestants. Its significance
lay in the fact that it was proof positive that Spain was
responding to the pressures of the Second Vatican Council and
to the public opinion of the rest of the world. In December

1964, Cardinal Quiroga, Archbishop of Santiago de Compostela, said:

> Religious liberty interests all the world. It inter-
> ests all of the hierarchy of the Church, including
> the Spaniards, in spite of the fact that the notices
> of the press and radio of some nations has desired to
> give the impression that we are not excessively inter-
> ested in it. It interests us because we know the
> situation of the world, in which it is necessary that
> the Church give its word about this question so impor-
> tant, religious liberty" (*Ya*, December 2, 1964).

In spite of the spectacular progress being made in Spain in the areas of industry, tourism, and the production of electrical power, Spain realized that she must have a better relationship with the rest of Europe if she were to survive. An effort was made to become an "associate" member of the European Common Market. This bid was blocked by the Scandinavian and Benelux countries on ideological grounds. There was reluctance on their part to support the intolerable conditions of Franco's Spain. No doubt the visit of Eugen Gerstenmaier, President of the West German Bundestag, to Spain to discuss the possibilities of Spain's entrance into the European Common Market helped influence the thinking of Spanish officials concerning religious liberty. Mr. Gerstenmaier was also a member of the Synod of the Evangelical Church of Germany and took the opportunity to talk with the Protestant leaders of Spain. At a press conference he stated that the "treatment of the problems of Protestants in Spain is 'the touchstone of Spain's earnestness' in joining the other European nations in efforts like the Common Market" (Henry 1964:665). Later, in his meeting with Franco, it was made quite clear that Spain would not be acceptable to the rest of Europe if religious freedom were not given to the Protestants. Franco spoke of the bill being proposed to grant such freedom, but clearly emphasized that there would be no freedom to proselyte. To this Mr. Gerstenmaier was reported to have pointed out that denial to evangelize was an infringement upon Christian liberty.

In March 1964, a landmark case in the legal history of Spain was reported. The Supreme Court ruled against the government and authorized an Evangelical church in Valencia. The court ruled that the government had erred in a ruling in 1961 when it barred the church's formation. Some evangelical leaders said that the decision was of the "greatest importance" (Commission 1964:31).

There could be no doubt now that the formal Ecumenical
Movement, world opinion, and the political-economic power of
Europe were having an effect on the situation of the Protestants
in Spain. A poll run by the Spanish Institute of Public Opinion
in 1965 to determine the attitude of the people in respect to
religious liberty, found that 67 per cent of the people were in
favor of total religious liberty in Spain.

Generalisimo Franco, in his New Year's address to the
nation in 1965, gave more encouragment. In words that clearly
echoed Pope Paul's Christmas message, he backed the Church's
concern along with the Vatican Council for "just and rightly
understood religious freedom." He assured the Spanish people
that they had nothing to fear from the present efforts to
broaden religious freedom and that they need have "no doubt of
suspicion about the exercise of freedom of conscience" (ABC
1964:1). It was now just a matter of time and the working out
of details before a religious liberty law would be passed.

The Law is Presented

On the 2nd of May, 1967, the Law of Religious Liberty was
presented to the Spanish Cortes (Parliament) for discussion.
It was introduced by the president of the Commission for Religious Freedom, Don Joaquín Bau, with these words:

> Spain recognizes that the world needs to be up-to-date
> both politically and spiritually ... Before there were
> those who wanted religious freedom without limits,
> outside of all moral and judicial norms. Following
> therefore the thinking of the Church that condemns that
> liberty, Spain adjusts her conduct to it, faithfully,
> firmly. Today, this liberty is concrete, assuredly,
> within the bounds of natural right and the law of the
> Kingdom of Spain, in this proposed law that we are
> going to examine (Monroy 1972a:20).

The proposed law was debated back and forth until the
eleventh of May when the final text was approved. The last day
of debate ended quite late and covered a good bit of ground.
Some said that the Cortes had received orders to finish quickly,
as the world was anxious to know the result. Others said they
were just tired of so much discussion. Whatever the reason,
the debate was over and an agreement had been reached.

A little over a month later all was ready. On June 26, 967, Don José María Oriol, the Minister of Justice, presented he law to the full assembly of the Cortes for the final vote ith these words:

> Honorable Lawmakers:
> The responsibility that falls to us in the elaboration and approval of this law is not hidden from me.
> I recognize the difficulties that it offers for various reasons: the newness it encloses; the dangers for Catholic unity some have believed to discover in it; the difficulty and even incompatibility of its coexistence with the confession of the State, that from opposite positions have been laying the blame, the polemic atmosphere that it has provoked, being a live issue; the climate at last reconciled, agitated extremely, on the one side, by those advocates of changes and new ideas, and on the other, by those remiss to walk in new paths that the Church presents to us.
> I believe that it falls to me, in the first place to clarify this profoundly disturbing misunderstanding about the incompatibility of the Catholic unity and the civil liberty in religious matters.
> I strongly, without the least bit of doubt or vacilation, declare that the civil liberty in religious matters that this law regulates, does not suppose the destruction of catholic unity that happily our country has reached, nor cannot present itself as radically incompatible with it ... (Monroy 1972:25).

When the count was completed, there were only nine negative otes and thus, on June 26, 1967, Spain passed a law regulating he meetings of non-Catholics. The Law of Religious Liberty ad become a reality.

3

THE LAW OF
RELIGIOUS LIBERTY

The passage of the Law of Religious Liberty ushered in a new day for Spain. All through the world the news of the law was received with joy and acknowledged as a major step forward for the country. The law is much too long and complicated to reproduce here, but a few of the major provisions will help in understanding its scope.

Article I
1. The Spanish State recognizes the right to religious freedom founded on the dignity of the human being and assures everyone the necessary protection, and immunity from all coercion in the legitimate exercise of said right.
2. The profession and practice, private and public, of whatever religion shall be guaranteed by the State without other limitations than those established in article two of this Law.
3. The exercise of the right of religious liberty, conceived according to the catholic doctrine, has to be compatible in all cases with the confession of the Spanish State proclaimed in the Fundamental Laws.
Article III
Religious beliefs shall not constitute a reason for a lack of equality for Spaniards before the law.
Article IV
All Spaniards, apart from their religious beliefs,

have a right to perform any work or activity, equally
to fulfill responsibilities or public office according
to their merit and ability, without other exceptions
than those established in fundamental laws or approved
norms.
Article VII
    The State recognizes the right of the family to
freely govern its religious life under the guidance
of the parents and recognizes their right to religious education to be given to their children.
Article XII
    Non-Catholic foreigners, whether resident or tran-
sient in Spain, in religious matters shall enjoy the
same rights and responsibilities as related to
Spaniards in this Law in all points where applicable
to them.

More details of the provisions of Article XII and the
relation it has to missionaries in Spain is given in Chapter
IV. In this chapter the effect of the Law is studied as it
relates to the State, the Catholic Church, and the Protestant
Churches.

THE EFFECT OF THE LAW ON THE STATE

From the very first mention of religious liberty in Spain,
those who opposed it argued that it would be detrimental to the
unity of the State. The Catholic Church proposed this argument
time and again, publically and privately. Archbishop Alonso
Muñoyerro of Sión, one of Spain's conservative prelates, said
that full religious liberty in Spain would enslave the conscience of the country's Roman Catholic majority and destrov
the Catholic unity in Spain (Christian Century 1965:788-90).

This fear was not only propagated by the majority of the
leaders in the Catholic Church, but had become the focal point
of the conservative political leaders also. During the debate
to approve the law in the Cortes, the dominate theme of the
opposition was to preserve the unity of the State. Sr. Barcena
expressed it this way: "We do not fear religious liberty, but
that our unity will be undermined by harmful proselytizing."
Another member of the Cortes, Coronel de Palma, added: "In the
name of 30,000 persons that do not profess our religion, they
seek to limit the rights of the 30,000,000 catholics" (Monroy
1972:20-1). Even at the time of the final vote to approve the

Law, the Minister of Justice took special care to reassure the
Cortes that the Law would not in any way disrupt the unity of
the State.

It is still relatively early to try to access the effect
that the Law of Religious Liberty has had on the State. From
outside the country it has served to give Spain an esteem that
she did not have before. Significant strides have been made
in relation to joining the European Common Market and the whole
world seems to view Spain in a different light. It would even
appear that the Spaniard himself walks with his head just a
bit higher, knowing that his country is not regarded as medieval
any longer.

Those who have maintained that the religious unity of Spain
is necessary for the civil unity of Spain are wrong. When
Monseñor Zacarías de Vizcarra says:

> In Spain, the loss of religious unity is, in short,
> the loss of national unity, with the sowing of con-
> tradictory ideas, with the reappearance of regional
> separations, internal wars and the return of celtic
> individualism, that will end in direct or indirect
> foreign domination (Monroy 1967:22),

he is expressing a fear that has no basis. This has not happened
in other countries of the world and it will not happen in Spain.
The well-being of the country does not depend upon the well-
being of the Catholic Church and this should be understood by
the people. The Church and the State are two separate entities
and have separate responsibilities. It would be best for the
two to understand themselves as such. Franco himself has said
that the two cannot be allowed to contradict one another in
their ends (Ya, December 31, 1971:6).

It is more likely that the unity of the State will suffer
from the communist ideology prevalent among the students and
workers than from any other source. In recent years there have
been numerous disturbances agitated by the communists. The
universities have been closed, the workers have gone on strike,
and there has been unrest in general. This certainly has had no
link to the passing of the Law of Religious Liberty, to the
Protestant Church, or to Protestant thinking. To the contrary,
these disruptive influences have more often come through the

church that claims to be the protector of national unity.

The Protestants have proven themselves to be just as proud of their country as any Catholic. They continue to fulfill their military obligations (only two so far have abstained on the grounds of conscientious objections) and have not formed into political parties. They have been able to distinguish between patriotism and religious belief, something that the catholic has not yet comprehended.

It cannot be maintained that the Law of Religious Liberty has been injurious to the State in any way. If anything, it has given the country a new vitality. I would say from personal experience that the Spaniard is very capable of making intelligent decisions. They have strong personal convictions and opinions which they forcefully argue when aroused. Certainly they are not convinced against their will. Passing the law has not changed the people. It has only opened to them the opportunity of using their intellect to decide for themselves how they will respond to an issue of utmost importance.

Since the Protestants are religiously rather than politically oriented, the State need not fear them. Their messages from the pulpit are Scripturally based and designed to lead the people into a close relationship with Jesus Christ and to live better lives. I have never heard politics discussed in any way from the pulpit, nor have I known of a message being changed in any way because of the presence of a secret policeman in the audience. On the other hand, it is very common to hear prayers being offered on the behalf of those in authority, asking that God would guide them and protect them. Evangelicals have a deep concern for the good of their country.

THE EFFECT OF THE LAW ON THE CATHOLIC CHURCH

Catholic fear of Protestant proselytism was the overriding factor in the opposition of the Law of Religious Liberty by the Catholic Church. If the law is to have any effect on the Catholic Church, it will have to be in this area. The opposition to religious liberty has been strongest in the Catholic Church and it has been publically expressed over the years. The Archbishop of Tarragona, Benjamine Cardinal de Arriba y Castro, who pleaded with the Vatican Council that any plans for ecumenism also include a rebuke for proselytism, said that he

was in favor of freedom of worship for non-Catholics, "but
there must be no proselytism." One prelate from Madrid expressed it this way: "We cannot have the spectacle of a minority
uprooting a minority faith." The Denver Catholic Register also
expressed this as the major fear of the Catholic Church in
Spain. It reported the activities of a missionary handing out
tracts in the city of Santander, a northern resort city and the
home of the Menéndez y Pelayo International University. The
article mentions that the tracts were printed in the United
States by the American Tract Society and were being distributed
by American "sects" in violation of Spanish law. The author
claims that "these activities will do more harm than good, both
to Spanish Protestants and to the cause of religious freedom.
Proselytizing in the streets is neither a Spanish nor Catholic
custom and is regarded as annoying" (August 11, 1965). Another
attack was directed at evangelistic efforts in the city of
Seville. "There are Protestants," said Cardinal Bueno y
Monreal, Archbishop of Seville,

> who not content with professing their belief, try to
> bring the apostacy of our less sophisticated brethren
> by gifts and promises of material benefits, and attack
> the Eucharist, the Virgin Mary or the Pope.

He also mentioned the high moral qualities and sincerity of the
majority of the Protestants and called for charity in dealing
with our "separated brethren." "The Spirit of God," he said,
"is fruitful in them also" (American, April 11, 1964:503).

There have been others, however, who have accused the
Protestants of offering gifts, material or financial, to win
converts. One Jesuit even goes so far as to say that the
missionaries who have gone to Spain are not the cultured Protestant of Europe, but are hostile fanatics, of little intellect,
who are agressive "proselyters" (Bravo 1965:4). His observations seem to be a bit harsh and unfounded, but do nevertheless
reveal some of the fear that the Catholic Church has of an
active evangelistic effort on the part of the Evangelicals.

Perhaps it would help if we examined the common use of the
word *proselyte*. Today the word usually conveys the idea of
persuading a person to change from one christian group to
another. Sheep stealing is often a standard way of expressing
the practice. This, however, is not what the word meant in the

New Testament. A proselyte, in the New Testament usage of the
word, meant a full-fledged convert to Judaism. It was a person
who not only accepted Jewish beliefs but also conformed to
Jewish customs as a new way of life (Galatians 5:3). The person may have been of a different race or country, but he became
a member of equal standing, religiously and nationally, with
those who were born Jews. This was the only way in the Jews'
eyes that a person could become part of "God's chosen people."
This concept was carried into the early church and quickly
became a point of contention. In Acts 15 the discussion centered around the problem of Gentiles becoming Christians. Did
they have to become Jews culturally in order to be Christians?
Paul ran into difficulties with his Jewish brethren when he
maintained that Greeks could become Christians on the basis of
their belief apart from adopting the culture of the Jews.

It was this same important point that was a vital ingredi-
ent in Luther's thinking. He objected to Germans being forced
to adopt a foreign cultural pattern. To be sure, he states his
concerns doctrinally, but the real issue of the Reformation was
as much cultural as theological. In the 16th Century the Roman
Catholic Church was propagating the idea that to become a
Christian was to adopt the Roman Catholic cultural tradition.
On the other hand Luther was contending for a church that could
be culturally German.

In Spain today the issue is basically the same. Can
Spaniards become, or be called, Christians who are not Roman
Catholics? The Protestants, according to their best theology,
do not insist that a certain cultural tradition is essential,
along with faith in Christ to be a Christian. If they do, they
deserve the label "proselyters." But if they remain true to
their traditional interpretation of scripture, they will avoid
what the Bible calls proselytism whether or not they can avoid
being called proselyters by moderns who are unaware of the
force of the New Testament at this point.

Just as there were special considerations given in the Law
to protect the unity of the State, there were also measures
taken to protect the privileged position of the Catholic Church.
The Archbishop of Sión, Alonso Muñoyerro, said: "I can say that
today, thanks to God and our leaders, it is not to be feared
that they (the Protestants) will pass the reasonable limits of
liberty" (ABC, December 17, 1964). In the Cortes there were

those who saw that these words were not uttered in vain. The
Marqués of Valdeiglesis, during the debate on May 8, 1967,
said: "Propaganda or proselytism cannot be admitted more than
with certain conditions, with determined shades." And Coronel
de Palma said: "It is necessary to impede at all cost the dif-
fusion of errors among catholics." Perhaps the most revealing
statement was that of the Baron de Carcer who stated: "We are
doing a favor, to concede a right to a small minority. But we
are not going to be stupid. The Catholic religion has some
privileges. Our situation is privileged" (Monroy 1972a:21).
There is no doubt that the Catholic Church in Spain is a privileged church and intends to stay that way.

The legalization of the Protestant Church in Spain has not
had an adverse effect on the Catholic Church. Those protesting
religious liberty on the grounds that it would cause the Catholics to be led astray by the Protestants were just attempting
to cover up a serious problem already existing in the Catholic
Church. A spiritual crisis, as described by the Catholics
themselves, was well underway. A writer named G. L. de la Torre,
writing in the Catholic Action journal *Signo* for January 28,
1950, states:

> Geographically we are witnessing a retreat of Cathol-
> icism. The faith has been losing ground in Spain.
> How long has this situation existed? It is the result
> of a slow process. Faith does not generally change
> into disbelief in a matter of hours ... The anti-
> religious fury of the Civil War did not arise spon-
> taneously, in a few hours or months. It was rather
> like a storehouse of explosives, accumulated over a
> long period of years which exploded when the time
> came. The great mass of workers deserted the house
> of God, and this did not happen suddenly. The suburbs
> of our large cities are almost solid blocks of
> irreligious feelings. The same can be said of the
> mining and industrial areas. On a much smaller scale,
> the same phenomenon can be observed in the middle,
> and even the upper class ...

Several books and many magazine articles have been written
expressing the same concern; the lack of spiritual interest on
the part of the people. Indifference, and even paganism are
words used to describe the situation where villages of fifteen

and twenty thousand people have only one church and it is never
full. The Bishop of Valencia, lamented the fact that only 17
per cent of his parish can be considered as faithful Catholics.
There have also been the surveys among the workers and the
university students revealing large numbers who have lost
interest in the Church with only 7.6 per cent attending the
Sunday mass. José Luis Aranguren sums up the situation with
these words:

> Our time is close to dechristianization, for religious
> indifference, for the lack of god. We are passing a
> 'dark night': God is without a doubt here, but the
> men of our time have scarcely given us the feeling of
> more than his bones, in the emptiness, in his absence
> (Monroy 1958: 37-38).

Some have gone so far as to call Spain a mission field for the
Catholic Church. The Protestants certainly have not been responsible for this situation, but they may very well be one of
God's remedies. When it is realized that the Christian faith
is not a cultural heritage, but a personal encounter with Jesus
Christ, there will be hope. Right now many Spaniards are saying no to religion and are not being given the opportunity to
say yes to God. Protestants in Spain desire to proclaim Christ
in a positive manner.

The continued prejudice against the Protestants undoubtedly has some of its foundation in the misuse of the word
"Protestant" itself. The Catholic Church has continued to use
the word in its present day context and has neglected the real
meaning. Today Protestants are considered to be a group which
originated in the 16th century in protest against the Roman
Church. The word "Protestant" actually comes from the famous
Protest offered against the decree of the Diet of Spires in
1529. Those who protested the Roman Churches reinterpretation
of a unanimous decision reached at the previous Diet in 1526
were called Protestants (Babington 1971:50). The problem
centered in whether religious convictions were to be the
decision of the individual or the authorities. The Protestants were willing to fight if necessary, to see that noone
would be forced by arms to adopt a certain religion. In Spain
the Protestants prefer to be called Evangelicals because of
the misuse of the word Protestant today. They want to be able
to demonstrate that they have a significant contribution to
make to their country.

It may very well be that the Catholic Church in Spain will learn a lesson from the advancement of the Protestants in Latin America. Instead of considering them as competitors, they should take note of the words of a Jesuit priest in Peru. He says:

> It may be one of the ironies of history that the final contribution of Latin American Protestantism will have been to awaken and revitalize a dormant Catholic Church. If indeed it does awake and come to life, it will not be because the Church rose from slumber to fight a hostile force, as in the days of the Reformation, but because that new force taught the Church urgently needed lessons about what its own prime task in the future must be (Klaiber 1970:102).

The indifference of the Spanish people to religion should cause careful reevaluation of the emphasis and actions of the Church in the past. The answer to the spiritual crisis in Spain today is not to deny the people a chance to hear the Gospel, just because it is preached by another group, but to make the Gospel all the more available. The Law of Religious Liberty is a step in the right direction and can only bring good to the people of Spain.

THE EFFECT OF THE LAW
ON THE PROTESTANT CHURCH

As can be expected, the Law of Religious Liberty has had its greatest impact on the Protestant Church. After all, it was written especially with them in mind. Listed as Law 44/67, it gave the Protestants new life and hope. Under the provisions set forth, the Protestant churches had until May 31, 1968 to register with the government. While reaction to the law was immediate, it wasn't all joyful. Three of the best known groups, the I.E.E., the I.E.R.E., and the U.E.B.E. objected to the law and refused to register under its provisions. Their objections were mainly centered in two points of the law. One was the requirement that a register had to be prepared by each church listing its members, and the second point dealt with the necessity of each church having its financial records accessible to the government. For the record here, those who decided not to register listed their objections as:

1. The law submits the churches to judicial structures
   which are inadequate for the principles of these
   religious communities.
2. Religious liberty is dependent on the practical
   administration and the discretion of executive
   power.
3. The law and the norms that complement it establish
   a system of unnecessary controls which are a clear
   discrimination against non-Catholics, especially
   those that refer to places of meetings and services
   of a religious nature.
4. The legislation acted, being moved by a lack of
   confidence inspired by the non-Catholic Spaniards,
   convinced that they would make bad use of the
   liberty; this explains the restrictive critera
   that appeared in the final version of the law, cut-
   ting to the limit the openings of the first pro-
   posals, that of the Ministry of Foreign Affairs
   (1964) and that of the Interministerial Commission
   (1966) (Albertos 1968:57-8).

To be honest, it must be said that none of the Protestant
groups were completely satisfied with the law as it finally
appeared. It was a bit ambiguous in some areas and did not
grant the liberty that was expected in light of the declaration
of the Second Vatican Council, but most were willing to accept
it as a significant step forward. At least it was better than
what they had before. By the end of 1971 all of the I.E.R.E.
churches, almost half of the U.E.B.E., and two of the I.E.E.
churches had reversed their position and decided to register
with the government. The advantages of being registered have
been found to outweigh the disadvantages. I believe that a
great many of the early fears about the law have now proved to
have been unfounded and that the majority of the Spanish Protestants are reasonably satisfied with the law.

The Spanish government was in a rather unpleasant situation
before the passing of the law. They had committed themselves
to the position of only admitting the existence of one church--
the Holy Roman and Apostolic Catholic Church. Now they were
faced with another group seeking recognition as a church. The
solution was that the Protestants have to register their churches
as businesses. They are provided for under a special category
restricted to religious organizations. This provides the legal

rights that have been needed and, at the same time, gave the
government some basis for dealing with them. All legal matters
are conducted through the office of the Evangelical Service of
Legal Assistance in Madrid. Although it is not officially recognized, it has been a satisfactory method so far. This is due
mainly to the outstanding ability of the Secretary, José Cardona.

One of the important provisions of the law is that which
allows the Protestant churches to own their own property. Formerly this was not allowed and property was in the name of a
mission agency or put into the name of individuals, a very
unsatisfactory situation. The new provision should have a good
effect on the churches in the future and may relieve some of
the tensions between mission agencies and local churches.

In the spring of 1971, I sent a questionnaire to all of
the foreign missionaries (couples were counted as one) that I
knew of in Spain. Among the questions was one in reference to
the effect of the Law of Religious Liberty on their work. Forty-
two out of the one hundred answered. The most frequent observation of these was that the law had indeed been helpful, especially in the area of evangelization. They felt that the people
received them more openly than had been true in previous years.
They also felt that the opportunities open to them were far
greater. The one negative observation mentioned most frequently
was a fear that the churches might relax their guard in light of
the new liberty and lose their witness rather than increase
their efforts.

The fact that Protestants are now legally recognized by
the government has done much to raise their prestige among the
people. There is still some of the stigma of the past, but
there have been many changes for the good. If there are not
substantially more baptisms taking place in the Evangelical
churches now, it can be doubted that the churches are taking
advantage of the liberty that they have. A few years have now
passed since the passing of the law and it is now time to begin
to analyze the situation objectively. A few years ago Jacques
Delpech estimated that there would be substantial numbers of
"crypto-Protestants" who would join the churches once there
was freedom to do so (1955:109). Has this happened? Is this
an explanation of one pastor's claim that Evangelism in Action
has recorded more conversions in one year than one denomination
has had in the previous hundred years (Gil 1970:17)? Does this

have anything to do with the substantial increase in the number
of new churches being formed throughout the country? During
1971 forty-five new groups were legally recognized by the Ministry of Justice, and probably a good many more too small to be
recognized were also begun. The potential is great and there
is an indication of an evangelistic spirit active among the
existing churches. An in-depth study of the patterns of growth
needs to be conducted soon.

All indications are that the past five years have been the
best in the history of the Protestants of Spain, and it appears
that they have only passed over the threshold of a whole new
era of growth.

THE EFFECT OF THE LAW
ON THE ECUMENICAL MOVEMENT

The Law of Religious Liberty did not spawn the ecumenical
movement in Spain. For some time there had already been a
handful of those who looked towards a day when Protestants of
various kinds as well as Catholics could dwell toghether in peace.
Many groups were represented in this thinking and they were
greatly encouraged by the events of Vatican II. This was the
time when a great new ecumenical wind blew across the world and
great things were being promised by those involved in the Prot-
estant/Catholic dialogues.

In Spain, while some Evangelicals dreamed idealistically
of a future day of union, the more realistic were contending for
some sort of better mutual understanding and acceptance. How
could there be dialogue between two groups when one was condemned
as in error and illegal before the talk began? The Second
Pastors and Evangelical Workers Conference held in Madrid in
1965 made it clear that the Evangelicals considered religious
liberty a prerequisite to ecumenical activities. This same
attitude is reflected in the official communication released
to the foreign (not local) press where it was stated:

> The relations that the ecumenical movement has brought
> about among the different confessions, Christian
> churches and nations of the world cannot but favor
> mutual respect, comprehension and understanding among
> all Christians. The Conference realized the benefits
> of ecumenical relations, but laments that they are
> impractical when official religious discrimination exists
> (Poveda 1965:59).

On the other hand, the official release to the Spanish press
omitted the last clause about religious discrimination. This
omission probably did little good as the Spanish press did not
print a statement about the Conference anyway.

For the most part the ecumenical spirit was advancing
among only a few. The hierarchy of the Catholic Church, while
not hostile, were certainly cool towards the idea of letting
Protestants gain too much ground. Likewise, the more conservative Evangelicals were sceptical that anything good would
come out of Rome. It was a situation that seemed doomed to
failure before it began. Among the Evangelicals the I.E.E. and
I.E.R.E. have been the two groups most interested in promoting
the ecumenical movement in Spain. Carmen Irizarry divides the
Protestants into two distinct camps when it comes to the ecumenical question:

> On the one side stands the Episcopalian, I.E.E.
> faction, open to dialogue, intellectually conditioned
> and more or less willing to forgive and forget the
> injuries of Spanish Catholics; on the other loom the
> so-called 'Fundamentalist' denominations - Baptists,
> Plymouth Brethren, Adventists, and Pentecostals -
> whose orientation is basically negative where inter-
> faith contacts are concerned (1966:237-38).

Her description displays her particular bias, but does certainly
divide the Evangelicals at the right place. However, the
"Fundamentalists" to whom she refers actually would probably
say that they do not so much oppose dialogue as they find it
to be of little value, since there is no real basis of unity as
things now stand.

In 1962 a small nucleus of priests, seminarians, and professors in Salamanca joined together to form an ecumenical
center. Named the Círculo Ecumenista Juan XXIII, it was dedicated to ecumenical action, information, and orientation. At
first there was general apathy as far as the ecumenical movement was concerned, but as it became evident that a Declaration
of Religious Liberty was going to be made by Vatican II,
interest picked up. Other centers have been formed in Barcelona
and Seville with small interest groups in various parts of the
country. For a short period an annual week of meetings was
sponsored jointly by Catholics and Protestants to foster better
relations and understanding. In the middle 60's these meetings

were well attended by both sides and even by both groups of
Protestants, but soon dwindled to almost nothing and in 1971
were discontinued. There have been some elaborate functions
held to generate more interest but they have left the conservative Evangelicals both untouched and unimpressed. The report
of the four day National Theological and Pastoral Conference
on Ecumenism held in Majadahonda in January 1970 reveals the
state of the ecumenical movement in Spain. The conference

> clearly marked the end of an initial stage of
> ecumenical euphoria in Spain and the beginning of
> a new period which will require greater depth of
> reflection and actions of the development of an
> ecumenical perspective achieved in the attitude of
> the diocesan ecumenical delegates throughout these
> past years ... (Vall 1971:214).

The ecumenical pot has been put onto a back burner for
awhile at least. There will be continued contacts on the personal and individual level certainly, but I do not see a significant movement in the near future. Actually, the Law of
Religious Liberty has had little positive effect on the ecumenical movement. There may be a legal acceptance of the Evangelical churches as businesses or associations, but the Catholic
Church is not ready to accept them as churches. Until this
happens, their meetings will be little more than the polite
shaking of hands, nervous conversation and a parting of the
ways again.

4

THE EVANGELICAL IMPERATIVES

As a minority group in Spain, the Evangelicals have many difficulties yet before them. This does not present anything new, but it does call for some careful evaluations of how they should move forward in the coming days. In this chapter, I present what I consider to be four imperatives for the Evangelical Church in Spain.

TO BE AN ACCEPTED CHURCH

The struggle for legal recognition by the Spanish government has at last become a reality for the Protestant Church in Spain. The provisions of the Law of Religious Liberty allow for the legal processes of law between the government and recognized churches. In cases where there has been need to resort to these measures, the judicial system has been fair to the Protestant group and the importance of this has been recognized and appreciated by those concerned.

The more difficult battle is still being waged. It is the struggle to be a socially accepted church. For this, there is no easy solution. Laws are not as effective in changing the more practical aspects of the day-by-day life on the street as one might desire. These changes take time and patience. Dr. José Cardona stated, at the time when the Religious Liberty Law became effective, that the Evangelicals of Spain would have five years in which to make their impact before indifference to

their cause would set in. If he is right, the time is quickly
coming to an end and much work remains to be done. Already
some of the advantages of being different have faded and the
hard climb out of social oblivion to acceptance is not complete.

The bright side of it is that significant strides have been
made in many areas and there is much hope. One such area has
been that of public officials who have willingly associated with
the functions sponsored by Protestants. An example of this was
the Annual Conference of the F.I.E.I.D.E. in 1971 at Caspe.
The Catholic mayor not only put in an appearance at the meetings,
he addressed the delegates and later was present for the closing
banquet. This type of acceptance has done much to break down
barriers of prejudice and indicates a changing of attitude on
the part of the many people. There has always been less stigma
attached to minority groups in the larger cities, but the breakdown of such stigmas in the smaller villages is of major importance.

To be recognized as first-class Spaniards by their fellow
citizens is important for the evangelical community of Spain.
In order for this to be accomplished, much ground will have to
be covered. One of the first steps will have to be an improved
image of the evangelicals by themselves. Having been an under-
ground church for so long has given a catacomb complex to some
evangelicals that hinders their acceptance. Becoming accustomed
to restriction and rejection has made it difficult to adjust to
toleration and new freedoms. Progress is being made rapidly in
this area and as more confidence is built up by successful experience, this will disappear. The more important necessity
for the Evangelical Church is that of being a relevant church.

TO BE A RELEVANT CHURCH

As was discussed in a previous chapter, the Catholic Church,
in spite of its place of privilege, has not retained the confidence of the working class and the students. It has only been
recently that it has become concerned with the life struggle of
the common people. In previous years the concern was for the
elite and ruling classes with the desire of retaining its position of power. Eugene Nida states:

In country after country, one finds the Roman Catholic
hierarchy concentrating on the elite, drawing its

principal leadership from this class, and seeing that
important members of the class feel no lack of education or spiritual assistance. At the same time, Roman
Catholicism has a wide appeal to the impoverished
masses, while among the middle classes there is often
a strong anticlerical sentiment (1967:31).

This expresses much of what has been true in Spain. For
years there were basically two social groups - the rich and the
poor. The Catholic Church appealed to the elite and thereby
was able to control the masses. It appears that the influence
on the elite has been little more than an indoctrination in
right thinking if the book *100 Españoles y Dios* is indicative
of their thoughts. It is an excellent example of a faithful
adherence to acceptable church doctrine in spite of a complete
lack of personal experience with God. The author, by means of
a frank questionnaire, asked one hundred famous Spaniards their
beliefs concerning God. The questions were:

1. Do you believe in God? If the answer is negative,
indicate the theory that satisfies you in respect to
the origin of the creation. In case of a positive
answer, indicate if you believe simply in a God-Creator,
of if you believe in a God that is also personal, that
is to say, related in some manner with man and with our
individual conscience.
2. Do you believe that there is something in us that
survives mortal death? (Immortal soul, rewards or
punishment, eternity).
3. Do you believe that Christ was God?
4. Do you believe that the Second Vatican Council has
been effective? (In case of a positive answer indicate
in what sense).
5. To what do you attribute the periodic persecution
of the Spanish Church, in a cruel way, by the people?
6. In what sense do you believe that science, tech-
nology and the intercommunication of people, will have
over the traditional Spanish religious feeling?
7. Have you had any personal experience (physical
sickness, psychological trauma, sensation of danger,
estacy or illumination, knowledge of exotic culture,
etc.) that might have influenced your actual religious
attitude (Gironella 1971:8)?

an eighth question was presented on an individual basis
according to the profession or circumstance of the person.
Usually it had to do with the relation of that person's
special field (art, music, economics, etc.) and religious
attitudes.

The answers given by these one hundred selected people
do not necessarily represent that of all Spaniards, but I
believe they do give an indication of the thinking or a great
many. The questions which were basically dealing with doctrine
were generally answered as any good son or daughter of the
Church would be expected to answer. Most would be considered
as "good Catholics". The next three questions were answered
in fairly predictable ways, and generally exhibited thought
and concern by the participants. The last question (No. 7)
was the one that sent them off in all directions. Only one
mentioned "conversion" as a religious experience that might
have influenced their actual religious attitude. Most considered some sickness, pain at the death of a loved one, dangers,
or other similar experiences as those having bearing on their
religious life. None claimed to have any type of personal
experience with God that Evangelicals would define as the
"new birth". A personal, living relationship with God was
apparently a foreign concept to them.

The Catholic anthropologist Luzbetak denies that the
Catholic Church has a policy of concentrating on the elite of
a country. Yet he says that the Church has just been wise in
recognizing that the elite are often the "powerhouse" of
social changes. He states:

> The official and wise teaching of the Church is
> rather to appreciate the special power and com-
> munication potential in whatever segment of the
> society it may be found (1970:300).

In Spain today, that would mean the new middle class. With
the growth of industry in the country, there is a large middle
class society developing, and it is very much outside the
control of the Catholic Church. This is a big concern of the
Catholics and it ought to be noted by the Evangelicals. The
following diagram shows the change that has taken place in the
development of the middle class from the year 1900 to 1960.
It is based on information derived from the *Instituto Nacional
de Estadística 1971:34.*

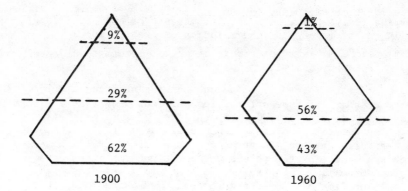

It is probably an oversimplification to divide the society into three divisions, but I have done it to show the degree of change that has taken place in a relatively short period of time.

According to Eugene Nida, the lower-middle and the upper-lower class have normally been the concern of Protestant missions (1972:104). It is this segment of society that represents the greates potential to the Evangelical Church and which should be actively sought. The rich will rarely respond, they feel that they have too much to lose, and the very poor may not come as they are afraid of losing their only known chance for salvation. It is the new middle class worker, merchant and student that should best respond to the doctrines of personal salvation, moral integrity, thrift, financial responsibility, and hard work. They have not lost the hope of improving their social position nor of seeing better things come about. The Evangelical Church needs to identify with the masses, recognize their needs and problems, and not be afraid to address itself to them.

The rapid progress of Protestants in Latin America has prompted studies to see how it came about. The most noted of these has been *Latin American Church Growth* by Read, Monterroso, and Johnson. When their study revelaed that the growth was taking place primarily among the Pentecostal churches, some people automatically tuned out, saying that the reasons were

because of their emphasis on healing and tongues. An emotional
religion appealing to an emotional people was what they claimed.
Those who did that have missed out on one of the most important
factors of church growth. Peter Wagner, an astute observer of
the Latin American situation has dug deeper and confirms what
Read, Monterroso, and Johnson first discovered; that the particular doctrines of the Pentecostals have not been the primary
factors responsible for their growth. Wagner states that "on
this score, the evidence indicates that, whereas doctrine un-
doubtably has something to do with Pentecostal growth, it by no
means is the only factor. It probably is not even the principal
factor"(1973:19). What then is the secret of their success?
The basic dynamic is the power of the Holy Spirit. They emphasize the Holy Spirit in their preaching, worship, conversations,
singing, and writing more than the other Evangelicals. Yet
while this is important, it is not the only factor. Wagner
says that "the Pentecostal doctrine of the Holy Spirit probably
is somewhat less significant than the Pentecostals like to
think, and somewhat more significant than the non-Pentecostals
like to think" (1973:17). This basic emphasis is combined with
methods that make their churches culturally relevant. Their
methods can and should be employed by all evangelical groups
concerned with reaching Latins. I have quickly summarized
eight of the factors that I feel should be utilized in Spain.

1. They are church-centered. (All converts unite with a
    local body.)
2. They are ardent church planters. (Mother-daughter
    principle.)
3. They sow in fertile soil. (The lower class in their
    case.)
4. The emphasize "body life." (The development and
    exercise of spiritual gifts among all believers.)
5. Their pastors are trained in the streets. (There is
    an apprentice program that develops pastors of the
    people.)
6. Their churches are culturally indigenous in their
    litergy. (The people think it is fun to go to church.)
7. They practice prayer for the sick. (More prevelent
    than tongues.)
8. They emphasize personal purity. (Not actively involved
    in social reforms as a church.) (Wagner 1973).

Number six of the list is one of the more important factors of

success and all those interested in church growth in Spain will
find this chapter worth the price of the book. The Evangelical
Church must be, above all, a relevant church.

Traditionally the Protestant churches of Spain have tended
to be mechanically conservative in theology. Adverse circumstances have not permitted them the luxury of theological dis-
putations that have engulfed the western churches. There have
been the normal differences in respect to doctrinal interpreta-
tions, but nothing sufficient to cause major disruptions, at
least not until recently.

The lack of Spanish Evangelical theologians has caused the
churches to look outside the country for its theological moor-
ings. These have come from Europe, and the Americas. Having
to fight for their very existence has kept their theology simple
and basic. The lack of theological seminaries has also served
to keep the contemporary theological discussions limited to
certain foreign-trained or influenced men. Of late the influence of German theologians has begun to be noticed, but still
only in limited circles.

With such close ties to the Latin American churches, it is
reasonable to expect that trends there will find their way into
Spain. The theological controversies of Latin America will no
doubt be noted if not joined by the Spanish Evangelicals.
Having both passed through periods when the Church was so busy
putting a soul-winning theology into practice that it had no
time to analyze it, they share a common need. Having no desire
to, and not being in a position to discuss theological trends,
it seems reasonable to suggest that missionaries and pastors
make themselves acquainted with the issues. A book that will
help in this respect is *Latin American Theology* by C. Peter
Wagner (1970).

There is a need for the Evangelical Church to have a theo-
logically relevant church structure for Spain. It is very
noticeable that the present structures are replicas of the
European and American denominational organizations. These have
been adopted and adapted to in a remarkable way, but I wonder
if they are what is functionally best for the country. Spanish
leaders need to examine afresh this area and make sure that it
represents their thinking and is Scripturally defensible. A
study of the Gypsy movement might be a revealing development
that can be helpful in seeing new possibilities.

Most of the churches have been using hymns translated from
English, and while they are generally well accepted, they do
not seem to touch hearts as music should. The hymn book of the
Brethren has been the most widely used in Spain and is comprised of translated hymns and is difficult to use by new
Christians. Learning how to use the hymn book is almost a part
of becoming a Christian in Spain. Since the Spanish are musical
and love to sing, it would seem that the development of national
talent should be encouraged and that new hymns should be written,
whether or not the missionaries feel comfortable singing them.

No church that is relevant to its society can overlook the
needs of its people. Here it must be kept in mind that this is
a problem that needs to be dealt with by the Evangelical Church,
not the missions. As foreigners and guests within a country,
the missionary must always use restraint, no matter how closely
he is associated with the people, in suggestion or encouraging
social changes. The area of concern for the missionary must be,
above all, the souls of men. But the role of the Church is
broader and includes the responsibility of social concern. In
Spain there are many areas of concern and that will have an
effect on the growth of the churches.

The political situation of Spain is one that is of constant
concern to the Evangelicals. There is always the speculation
about what will happen with the passing of Franco and how the
Church will be affected. His close association with the Catholic
Church has been the cause of some discontentment and agitation
among the working class. How the Evangelical churches identify
with the people will unavoidably have some political implications.
In seeking to win the workers to Christ, suspicion will be
aroused as to the motives, as the Catholic Church has used them
for political motives before. That the political position of
the Evangelicals is a personal matter needs to be stated here
again so that it can be seen in the light of the whole church.
While the choice is individual, the society will tend to view it
corporately. The impression transmitted to the society must be
determined by the Spanish Christians, not the missionaries.

The rise of Communist activity in Spain is a political
problem arising out of the social situation. Although it is an
unauthorized organization in Spain, it continues to grow. This
will have some effect on the Evangelicals. Having been falsely
associated with the Communists in the past will continue to

plague them. This will be especially true since they will be
trying to reach the same groups of people, although for different reasons. Some of the antichurch element may try to associate
with the Evangelicals, hoping to use the legal organization for
fighting the system. This was true in the 1930's and hindered
growth of the Evangelicals then. It must be avoided now. Any
sense of political orientation must be avoided even though they
might sympathize with the masses who feel exploited and who are
seeking a way to improve their situation. The greatest number
probably have felt the need in the economic realm.

Just as most of the countries of the world, Spain is experi-
encing the movement of the rural people to the cities. Widespread unemployment in the villages and especially in the areas
of Extremadura and Andalucia have caused many to move to the
urban centers seeking work. The economic miracles of the "technocrats" have improved the conditions of the country, but the
price controls and wage freezes have tightened the purse strings
of the people to a serious degree. A highly volatile situation
exists in many areas of the country.

This migration has its effect upon the Evangelical churches.
The village churches have the feeling of frustration and dis-
couragement. Just as it seems a person is becoming active, he
moves to the city to become a part of a growing congregation.
In the village the work seems hard and slow, while in the city
the impression is that the work is being "blessed" and grows.

The rapid increase of population into centers such as
Madrid and Barcelona creates new problems. The government is
trying to solve some of these by establishing satellite cities.
These are to be centers of industry away from the present industrial areas which will help in the distribution of the population. The map on page 63 shows the direction of movement among
the people during the past ten years. Basically, it is from the
central sections to the coasts and industrial centers.

Figure 5

DIRECTION OF MIGRATION IN SPAIN 1960-70

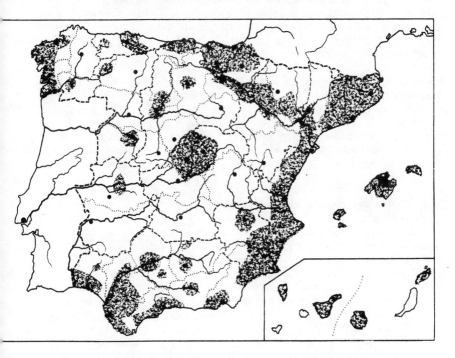

Areas of Decrease ☐   Areas of Increase ▓

One of the most startling phenomena of the Spanish migration pattern is the number of people working outside the country. Ten per cent of the population is working in a foreign
country. Over two million Spaniards are in Latin and North
America and over a million are in other European countries.
Argentina is the most popular in South America with 1,102,650,
while in France there are 616,750. The age group of these
migrants is that of the prime working years with 84.1 per cent
between 15 and 39 years of age (López 1971:28-33).

This large number of Spaniards in foreign countries represents a remarkable opportunity that is not being taken advantage
of to any degree. Most of the workers in Europe go to France,

Switzerland, Germany, etc., to earn money in quantities not
found in Spain. Usually they are men who leave their families
behind and go for a year or so before returning home. In the
foreign country the men live in ghetto-like communities. They
send back funds for the family and while this is a tremendous
help to Spain's balance of payments problem, it is hard on
families. Some of these men come under the influence of the
Gospel in these countries, but the temptations are tremendous
and the conditions under which they live are less than ideal.
This would seem to be a receptive homogeneous unit that could
be instrumental in the evangelization of Spain. The Spanish
government has anticipated this to some extent and in the
short course given to prospective migrants there is included
a short speech warning them to beware of dangerous new ideas
about the nature of government and the Church (Aceves 1971:
116).

Those who may be considering a new area of work should
take into consideration the movement of the people. New
missionaries should not make the mistake of thinking that just
because there is no work in an area that it is a good place to
go. It is probably just the opposite, and that is why no one
is there. It will be noted from the chart on pages 21-22 that
the provinces of Guadalajara, Soria, Segovia, and Teruel have
not had an evangelical work since before 1933, and probably
not before then either. These are difficult areas. Guadalajara,
for example, has had at least two attempts in the past, but to
no avail. No doubt the other provinces are just as difficult.
I personally believe that Segovia is becoming less resistant as
personal visits to the capital of that province have indicated
at least a mild interest.

The fact of migration should not necessarily be a handicap
to Evangelical churches. If they can adapt themselves to meet
the needs of these socially dislocated masses, they will become
fast growing churches. If they can offer answers to the pressing
needs and give hope while directing them to new values and
meaning to life, they will be fulfilling their responsibilities
and will be a relevant church.

TO BE A GROWING CHURCH

Since the Evangelical Church, at best, comprises only
one-tenth of one per cent of the population, there is a huge
task of expansion ahead. The past methods of multiplying

churches will not suffice in this day. Not only have they been
too expensive and time consuming, they have not been effective.
For example, to place a missionary or national couple in an
area by themselves to start a church can take years of time and
result in only a handful of faithful followers. Under present
conditions and methods, one hundred years would not be sufficient to reach half of Spain and we do not have that kind of
time.

Many of the churches of Spain have a history of stagnation.
There are various reasons to account for this. Some are legitimate, others are not. Taking into account the areas where just
maintaining a witness has called for much personal sacrifice
and devotion on the part of evangelical Christians, I would be
the last to criticize their faithfulness. This, however, is
not true of all areas and there are places where the lack of
growth is not the result of outside persecution, but the lack
of effective witness on the part of the Christians. To elimi-
nate the possibility that this will be interpreted as the attitude of a foreign missionary alone, I want to quote from some
of the leading national pastors. In a questionnaire asking
them to comment on "What are, in your judgment, our greatest
opportunities and gravest dangers?" and published in an article
entitled "The Evangelical Churches in the Light of Their Mission", these leaders voiced some excellent observations.
Humberto Capó, Secretary of the Spanish Evangelical Council
and Director of the evangelical school *El Porvenir*, said:

> I observe that in the 'small' evangelical churches of
> Spain, many have taken so much joy in the life of the
> closed circle of the church that they don't know how or
> don't care to leave it.

José Flores, the Director of the United Bible Society of Spain,
says:

> I see, from my watchtower in Madrid, two principal
> opportunities for the growth of our churches, these
> opportunities are two at least, that should permit,
> must permit, our leaving the pernicious 'ghetto'
> of a religious minority, that to which we cannot
> subject ourselves any longer. First, take the Law
> of Religious Liberty by the horns, that is to say,
> not to fear it. The Law is a lemon, given by God
> (or do we doubt His sovereignty?) and we have to

know how to squeeze it and put sugar on it. Without
obedience to the Law (I know that many discredit this
advice) we will be crippled for the way, and the
opportunities for certain churches will disappear.
Second, the 'openness' of the Spanish people to the
Bible, in which we must signal our faith and our
reason, and the openness toward the protestants,
which permits us an open and honorable dialogue to
indicate 'the way, the truth, and the life.

The last quote from the article, although there were many more
worth noting, comes from Juan Gili, President of "Evangelism
in Action." He says:

The first opportunity begins in the individual
believer, truly converted to Christ. This opportunity
does not have to do with time nor circumstances. A
good part of the contemporary Spanish evangelical community is the fruit of personal testimony, given in
difficult circumstances. I believe that if each one
of the miscounted thirty thousand 'protestants' were
to understand the significance of living 'in' and
'for' Christ and practiced it, this decade would be
the decade of the Spanish miracle of faith. The
other opportunity is to know how to apply the evangelistic strategy as much in ways, as in actual available methods in order to reach the masses, taking into
account, the urban development of certain zones of the
country by reason of the migratory movements. I do
not believe that they would reach 5%, the local
churches that in the three years of having more opportunities, have used them for this end. Those that have
and are doing it, already are gathering their fruit.
And those Christians are called to gather 'much fruit'
             (Carta Circular, Enero-Febrero, 1971:11-19).

Now that the government has given legal recognition to the
Protestants, and the people are becoming less opposed to them
socially, there can be no reason not to expect growth among
the evangelical churches. If they are not growing they need
to reexamine themselves to see if they are really availing themselves of the opportunities God has given, or if they have
sealed themselves off from the people.

For the Evangelical Church to grow in Spain, it will have to give careful consideration to new forms of evangelization and form a practical strategy. For the western missionary, this usually means some type of big campaign. Thousands of pieces of literature are distributed and as much publicity as can be generated are considered essential for such a program. In the past such activities were difficult, if not impossible, to execute. Laws did not permit such programs and the evangelical churches were not wealthy enough to support them. Today things are changing and various groups are attempting large-scale campaigns. There are still plenty of barriers to overcome and most attempts have encountered enough opposition to make them trying experiences. Some of the more successful attempts have been those of Evangelism in Action. They have embarked upon a program of renting theaters in various villages and cities and showing Billy Graham films free of charge. In this manner they have been able to fill theaters to capacity (many times over a thousand people) night after night. It is hoped that their success in gaining access to respected media will be instrumental in breaking down prejudices against the Protestants. The actual benefits in respect to church growth will not be known for awhile yet, and will not be substantial if a careful plan of follow-up is not used.

Some people have suggested that Dr. Billy Graham should conduct a campaign in Barcelona or Madrid. This has been considered, but I doubt that the time is ripe for such a large-scale effort. The Evangelical Church of Spain is in a critical period of transition and needs to solidify some before such a large-scale evangelistic program is attempted. Should such an attempt be made at this time, I believe that the amount of fruit conserved would not warrant the effort and cost. There exists a situation which is very similar to that of Latin America and the result of the Evangelism in Depth programs. Though well prepared and managed, the fruit of the program did not result in significant church growth. Dr. Peters discusses this phenomenon and gives some thoughtful possibilities to account for it in his study (1970:74-77). The evangelical churches of Spain are not prepared for a sudden influx of new believers. Until there is an ability to follow up and follow through with converts, there can be no large ingathering in Spain. Yet, a large ingathering is just what is needed.

The traditional method of individual conversion has to be augmented by group, multi-individual conversion patterns. This

has to be recognized as not only a possibility, but a necessity.
The outworkings of this will vary from place to place, but it
must be done. The advantages of group evangelism (family,
students, homogeneous units) are far more to be desired than
the disadvantages they involve. Dr. Peters lists the advantages
as:

1. Group evangelism and multiple conversions usually
make for greater personal health because the self-
image remains unimpared.
2. They aid greatly in breaking the non-Christian ways,
practices, mental images and psychological molds.
3. Group proceedings leave the individual in his web
of relationships; he is allowed and encouraged to live
a Christian life without fearing social, cultural or
economic ostracism or physical persecution.
4. Group evangelism and multiple conversions will
facilitate the social, cultural and spiritual uplift
of the people.
5. Group evangelism and multiple conversions make
self-government, self-support and self-propagation not
only a possibility but natural from the very beginning
of the Christian movement (1970:219-20).

Group evangelism will be different in the city than in the
village, but it should be done in both. Small villages which
are face-to-face societies (i.e.; everyone known everyone else)
tend to function as extended families. Such a village tends to:

(1) Make collective decisions, (2) have considerable
inner cohesion, (3) present a unified front against
intrusion, (4) be conservative in orientation, and
(5) be centralized in its control, in the pattern of
the family (Nida 1967:45).

In such a situation the logical approach would seem to be in
terms of winning the leadership first. If the leaders, be
they a ruling family, or certain respected elders, can be won,
the others will tend to follow. This would result in a large
group being converted and a church being established with a
minimum of difficulty. If, on the other hand, only one or two
young people, or disgruntled members of lower strata of society
are converted and they become the basis for your church, it is
unlikely that that church will ever become a vital and relevant

part of the community. It will be forced to win converts one
by one, ostracizing them from their families and causing social
dislocation. This is undesirable as people prefer to become
Christians without crossing social barriers.

Since it is doubtful that many villages in Spain are ready
to convert en masse, although there may be more such villages
like Teregoña, the Evangelical Church will continue to be a
minority group. As such, there will still be severe social
pressures upon it depending upon the size of the community in
which it is located, the composition of the group willing to
be associated with it, and the amount of pressure the Roman
Catholic priest can arouse against the intruding force.

Because most of the villages of Spain are face-to-face
societies, the bulk of the Protestant activities are in urban
areas. This seems to be following the same pattern as the
early church in the Roman Empire. Latourette speaks of this,
saying, "It is clear that the faith spread first in the cities
and that during the first three centuries it was predominately
urban rather than rural"(1971:110. The similarities between
the situation of the early church and the Evangelical Church in
Spain today in spite of the fact that it was illegal in Rome
and is legal in Spain, are so striking that I believe much benefit can be derived from a careful study of the methods of the
early church. After all, the early Christians were a minority
group trying to inspire discipleship in a pleasure-seeking,
materialistic, and outwardly religious society too.

Without laboring the point, I would like to point out four
of the most outstanding characteristics of the early church in
its expansion in the Roman Empire. These should also be characteristic of the Evangelical Church in Spain. First of all is
the total involvement of each church member. First century
Christianity was, above all, a lay movement. Secondly, the
community life of the early Christians was exemplary in love,
joy, and transformed living. Their infectious enthusiasm invited examination and emulation on the part of the world.
Thirdly, they had a deep sense of purpose. They were really
concerned that men and women without Christ were doomed to an
eternal death and needed to be saved. The urgency of the situation drove them to proclaim the good news fervently and widely.
Finally, they had a clear understanding of the message they
proclaimed and cultural and intellectual patterns that would
make that message more receptive. They understood the needs

and thoughts of the world in which they lived and applied their
methods with lasting results. Geographical factors were doubt-
lessly factors that led to the following of trade routes and
roads as the Jews had done before them. These routes and roads
led to the cities and the areas of greatest receptivity. Evangelicals in Spain are being forced into a very similar pattern.

In the cities, the social pressures are not as severe as
in the villages, but here the mistake should not be made of
carrying on with an individualistic type evangelistic program,
unless forced to do so. Whole families should be the aim as
well as other responsive homogeneous units. We should find out
what groups are more favorable to change and suit our methods
to their needs. We must know their frustrations, imbalances,
desires, and apply the Word of God to lead them to the One who
can comfort, guide, and satisfy. The groups most likely to be
receptive will be:

1. Those who are in a process of change. The people who
    have had an opportunity to become settled in and be-
    come established in a community will be more difficult
    to change.
2. New social groups. In a changing society, new groups
    are being formed. These will be more susceptible to
    change if presented with new information before be-
    coming established.
3. Groups in turmoil. People with felt needs (brought
    about by financial need, insecurity, social injustice,
    and health needs) are more open to change.
4. Groups that are looking for a change. There are always
    some people who are challenged by new ideas.

When you have established in your mind the group that you are
going to try to reach, you can then establish your lines of
communication. How can you relate to them with the least possible amount of offense? How can you meet their need? Your
attempts will meet with greater success if it is through group
penetration rather than confrontation. "Men like to become
Christians without crossing racial, linguistic, or class
barriers" (McGavran 1970:198). The fewer unnecessary barriers
that we place before men in winning them to Christ, the better.

It is time to begin to think of winning whole groups of
people to Christ in Spain. People movements are necessary and

desirable. That they are possible is clearly exemplified in
the Gypsy movement which is taking place at the present time,
but they do not happen by accident. A people movement needs to
be planned and consciously attempted. Because this is such a
radical departure from the normal program, we must look more
closely at what a people movement is. It is not the same as a
mass movement, nor the careless admittance into the church of a
large number of people. It is not the result of a missionary's
eager attempt to have a large number count to report to the
churches back home, nor does it result in nominal Christianity.
The fact is that people movements in the beginning stages are
not usually recognized as such. They may pass through a period
of time and often have to overcome many obstacles before be-
coming·acceptable to other Christian groups. What then is a
people movement?

> A people movement results from the joint decision of a
> number of individuals - whether five or five hundred -
> all from the same people, which enables them to become
> Christian without social dislocation, while remaining
> in full contact with their non-Christian relatives,
> thus enabling other groups of that people, across the
> years, after suitable instruction, to come to similar
> decisions and form Christian churches made up ex-
> clusively of members of that people (McGavran 1970:
> 297-8).

Once the Evangelical Church begins to focus in on receptive
homogeneous units with a relevant Gospel message, a people movement will be under way and the Evangelical Church will be a
fast-growing church, capable of fulfilling its responsibility
to the people of Spain.

TO BE A SELF-RENEWING CHURCH

The end of the Evangelical Church in Spain is not simply
to be a fast-growing Church. It must be a self-renewing church.
In order for this to be accomplished, there will undoubtedly
need to be a change in the present concept of the church. A
"good" church has usually been pictured as one with a full-time,
paid, seminary-trained pastor, a large attendance on Sunday,
and a nice building. It is this very image that has hindered
growth in many cases around the world and that is hindering
growth in Spain. The size and financial resources of the

average Spanish church does not allow for supporting a full-
time pastor, building and maintaining a large meeting place,
and carrying on an extensive evangelistic program. If this is
the criteria for determining a "good" church, then there are
few to be found. My findings lead me to believe that very few
churches in Spain are completely self-supporting. Foreign help
is being received to finance a building or a pastor, and in
many cases, both. Some churches may be able to support their
pastor, but few could finance a building at the same time. This
was a problem cited by García and Grubb in 1933 as one of the
causes for slow growth then. They said:

> Self-support is virtually unknown in churches with
> ministerial provision. As the salaries of the pastors
> are paid in most instances by foreign committees, the
> congregations, in their turn, have felt little respon-
> sibility towards their ministers. It is true that
> most of the congregations are extremely poor, but they
> have not yet begun to appreciate even the elements of
> self-support (1933:85).

This is still a problem and one that is not being faced up to
generally. I have had more than one pastor privately speak to
me about the need for increased emphasis on giving in the
churches. Although this is a need, it is not the solution completely. In many instances if the the congregations were to
give one hundred per cent of their income to the church, it
would still not be sufficient to support a pastor and finance
a church program on the scale thought to be desirable. The
need is for a changed attitude in regard to what constitutes
a church.

Because of the prevalent idea of what a church is, a program of reeducation will have to be undertaken. Niel Braun
expresses this need in the following way:

> The hardest task will be to convince Christians in
> small churches that they can be genuine and sound
> churches without a salaried pastor. If the clergy
> and the Christians in larger churches take the atti-
> tude that any church that amounts to anything 'of
> course' has a salaried pastor, then the task will be
> harder still (1971:93).

A "good" church should not be regarded as one that supports its own pastor, has a large attendance, and has a nice, modern building. There must be other criteria. How is that church reproducing itself? Are new groups being brought into being as a result of the efforts of its members, or is it spinning its wheels trying to be a "good" church? Is the church interested in extension growth or only concerned about expansion growth?

A church with an active program of evangelization, a series of preaching points, numbers of home Bible study groups, and an expanding Sunday School will quickly realize the need for training its own leadership. No school exists with the capabilities of supplying the amount of leadership needed at this moment, much less in the future, for growing churches and their programs. Active participation by the total church is a necessity and will call for a reevaluation of the present training methods. This leads us to another of the basic problems of church growth in Spain: the system of training pastors. The syndrome of a single, paid, seminary-trained, full-time pastor for every church has not worked successfully outside of the wealthy western countries and even there it is breaking down. It is a luxury that few can afford. In Spain there are not enough pastors to care for the established churches and the training programs are not producing others fast enough to meet the need. Not only are they not being prepared fast enough to meet the need, they are all too often being prepared for needs that do not exist. Part of this is because of a faulty concept of the ministry. The tragic dichotomy between those that serve and those being served has been carried over from the Catholic Church and perpetuated by the missionaries. The pastor is to minister and the laity are to be ministered to. This attitude will have to be corrected if the Evangelical Church is to become the vital, vibrant force for God in Spain that it ought to be.

These perennial problems of training pastors and determining the responsibilities of the clergy are ones that are being reexamined all around the world. In Latin America the success of the Pentecostal churches has been attributed, in part, to their success in solving these two problems. They are training their men to be church planters and they know what they are expected to do. Laymen are active in teaching Bible studies, preaching in the streets, and instructing new converts. Those that exhibit special abilities (gifts) are given greater responsibilities and by the time they become pastors they have become capable leaders. They are not just caring for a handful of believers, waiting upon their every need. They are now busy training their laymen in the skills of leading Bible studies, preaching, etc. They are not pastors by virtue of having completed a specific amount of time in a school, or because they have taken a certain number of courses, but because they are God's men for that place, and recognized as such by the people to whom they minister.

By and large, the theological schools in Spain today represent large investments of money for the training of small numbers of students. They are also financed, with few exceptions, by foreign funds. Needless to say, there has to be a better way of training leadership that is within the realm of possibility for the local congregations. This has been one of the strong points of the Brethren churches. Through correspondence courses and short term Bible Schools, they have been training their leaders in the churches. This has made it financially possible as well as locally practical. The result is that they have trained the leaders of the churches, not just "promising" young men that might or might not work out at a future date. The future growth of the Evangelical Church in Spain demands more training on the local level with the leadership of the churches being assumed by laymen.

In order to bring this about consideration should be given to Theological Education by Extension programs. This recent development in pastoral training has been successfully introduced into several areas of the world. Making training available on the local level has many advantages and should not be considered as a lowering of academic standards. It is rather a means of making good training more accessible to those who will gain the most from it at a price they can afford. It is also a means of helping the local church gain the benefits of trained leaders quickly. In Spain there will still be a need for a resident seminary system for those who can devote a period of time to the intensive program of study in an academic atmosphere and an extension school should be connected to a resident school. However, the emphasis should be upon the student need, not architectural excellence. Once the training programs become centered on people and functions instead of programs and forms, there should be a change in attitudes that will permit the Evangelical Church the freedom it needs to fulfill its imperative as a self-renewing church.

5

AN OVERVIEW OF THE EVANGELICAL CHURCHES

The rapid expansion of evangelical groups in Spain is most heartening. After all, this is why much time, money, and energy have been expended over the years. How and why churches grow are pertinent questions in these days and cannot be ignored by pastors or missionaries. How many people are coming into the churches, why they are coming, and in many cases why they are not coming should concern us as we consider the Evangelical Church as it exists in Spain today.

This chapter is devoted to the evangelical churches and their various service agencies. Little will be said about those groups which have come into being during the past few years if I have not been able to personally determine their origin and purpose. The first section deals with the organized denominations and associations of churches.

THE CHURCHES

Up until recently it was fairly easy to keep track of the various local churches and their affiliations. As late as 1961 there were only seven recognized associations of churches and an additional category referred to simply as Independents. To-day there are at least twenty-three organized groups of churches and many more independent churches throughout Spain. Keeping track of them and their affiliations has become almost impossible. During the years there have been groups started which

75

have since died out or become associated with other organizations and thus have lost their original identities. I will
not attempt to trace out and identify these for you except in
cases where it is of importance to know the old associations
in order to understand the new. The most logical manner of
presentation seems to be that of beginning with the oldest
groups and moving forward to the present. Only the six largest
groups are listed.

The Spanish Evangelical Church (I.E.E.)

Before the revolution of 1868 occurred in Spain, which was
to permit the entrance of Protestant workers into the country
again, there had been various attempts made in establishing
groups of believers, but with little success. This did not
discourage some however, and in Gibraltar Juan Bautista Cabrera,
a former priest, began to organize a band of exiled Spanish
Protestants. They prepared themselves for five months, praying
for the door to open for them to return to their country and
in April of 1868, the day came. Moving quickly, they spread
out into the country and it seemed as though Protestant communities began to spring up spontaneously all over Spain. The
principle center of operations was the city of Seville where
Cabrera labored to prepare a Spanish ministry. In 1875 he moved
to Madrid and it was there that the first Protestant assemblies
were held. Soon the various churches began to organize and in
1871 a "synod" was held with representatives from all over Spain
being present. Among the representatives two lines of thought
emerged: one in favor of a Presbyterian form of government and
the other in favor of an Episcopal form of government. The
majority of the churches formed the Spanish Christian Church,
but the union did not prosper and the various churches adopted
their own form of government.

In 1880 another "synod" met and the result was the formation of the Spanish Reformed Episcopal Church (I.E.R.E.). It
was comprised of three churches from Seville, one from Malaga,
and one from Madrid. Cabrera was elected as Bishop of the new
group. For all practical purposes, the split brought about the
formation of the I.E.E., although it was not formally called
such for another six years. It is comprised of churches of
Presbyterian, Methodist, Congregational, and Lutheran back-
grounds. According to Estruch, it is also the group which
represents the most genuine European reformed tradition, both
in form and doctrine (1967:32).

The I.E.E. has the country divided into four sections: the South, the Central, the Northeast, and the North. In 1970 they were reported to have 35 churches, 15 mission points, and 4,000 members (Saladrigas 1971:86). The following graph, Figure 6, is based upon figures given in the *World Christian Handbook* for the years 1952, 1962, 1968, and the final figure is that which is mentioned above. All graphs are done on logarithmic paper to give the true perspective of growth.

The Spanish Reformed Episcopal Church (I.E.R.E.)

The origin of this group has already been mentioned in connection with the I.E.E. However, its growth in numbers of churches and in membership has not kept pace with its sister group. In 1961 it was comprised of twelve churches and 697 members. The membership increased to 1,100 by 1968 while the number of churches remained the same. The number of churches listed in the figures released by the Evangelical Legal Assistance Service at the end of 1971 placed the number of churches at 15 and I would estimate that the membership would be close to 1,500. The I.E.R.E. was one of the groups which declined to register with the government under the provision of the Law of Religious Liberty when it was effectuated in 1967. It did change its mind in 1971 and has now registered all fifteen of its congregations. The growth chart for the I.E.R.E. is Figure 7.

The Plymouth Brethren

Although this group of churches was probably heavily dependent upon missionary help in the days of the Second Reformation (the late 1800's), it has since become a strong force with practically no outside help. The strong autonomy of each church, as well as their reluctance to keep membership roles, has made it a bit difficult to determine the exact size of the Brethren Church.

The Brethren have been strong in their development of "elders" within the local church situation and have developed a fund for the support of certain men recommended by the elders as capable of full-time service. The fund began around 1949 when there were five such men set aside for the ministry. The amount of money given by the various churches throughout the country has risen from twelve thousand pesetas in 1950 to

seven hundred and thirty thousand pesetas (over $10,000 under
present exchange rates) in 1965. During the same period of
time the number of full-time workers increased from five in
1949 to fifteen in 1965 (Valbuena 1965:18-19). Although I do
not have access to figures as to the amount contributed to the
fund in recent years, I am sure that it has continued to increase, especially in light of the fact that in 1965 there
were some 60 Brethren places of worship and in 1971 there were
95. The Brethren constitute the largest evangelical group in
Spain at the present time. The figures given by the *World
Christian Handbook* for 1952, 1962, and 1968 are put into the
graph showing the growth of the Brethren. (See Figure 8.)

The Southern Baptist (E.U.B.E.)

The next largest evangelical group in Spain is the Southern
Baptist. The Baptists' work originated with William Knapp, who
arrived in Madrid in 1869. He had apparently gone to Spain in
1867, but for the first two years he worked as an independent.
By 1870 he was reported to have founded five churches, among
them the first Baptist church in Madrid. On April 5, 1870 he
reported that he and his Spanish worker had had 1,325 pro-
fessions of faith in a seven month period. Mr. Knapp left in
1876 and the work was continued by Eric Lund. In 1882 the
Northern Board (of the U.S.A.) took over the work, and continued with it until the Baptist World Alliance in 1920. It was
then that the Southern Baptist Convention became officially
responsible for the work in Spain. In 1922 there were reported
to be 600 Baptists in Spain (Hughey 1964:49). It was not until
1928 that the Spanish Convention came into being officially and
was called the *Unión Evangélica Bautista Española* (U.E.B.E.)

Probably the Southern Baptists have the best records available for being able to check their progress. The book *The
History of the Baptists in Spain* by David Hughey gives their
history up until about 1955. It is not necessary to repeat that
history here, but perhaps a few of the highlights would be helpful. In 1936, at the beginning of the Civil War, there were
1,054 members of the Baptist churches of Spain. Hughey reports
that in 1939, at the end of the War, that the only Baptist
Church able to function in a more or less normal way was the
one in Madrid (1964:74). Things improved gradually and by 1947
a pastors' conference (nine churches were represented) expressed
a desire to the mission that the churches be permitted to

govern, propagate, and sustain themselves. Since that time
there has been a degree of autonomy on the part of the local
churches. In 1947 courses by correspondence were begun for
the training of ministers and in 1948 the seminary was opened.
In 1955 the Ladies Missionary Union formed a home for old
people. Using the figures of Hughey and the *World Christian
Handbook* (a request for the exact figures was not answered)
the growth chart for the Southern Baptists is as follows on
Figure 9.

The Federation of Independent Evangelical Churches of Spain

The Federation of Independent Evangelical Churches of
Spain came into existence on the 9th of January 1957. Nine
churches met at a church in Barcelona and adopted a Constitution, Statutes and a Declaration of Faith. The idea was to
give the various independent churches an organization which
would allow them to retain their autonomy and yet have a way
of cooperating in projects and plans that could only be accomplished by more than one church. To the original churches,
thirty-one others have joined the F.I.E.I.D.E. to make it the
fourth largest evangelical group in Spain. The following
chart, Figure 10, is made up from figures given to me by the
F.I.E.I.D.E. and are, therefore, very accurate.

The Evangelical Gypsy Movement

Since the early 1950's there has been an evangelical
movement gaining ground among the Gypsies of Europe. France
has been the center of this with some 10,000 baptized members.
The movement moved into Spain by means of Gypsies converted in
France who returned to Spain (Barcelona). Later some were
sent to the Madrid area and in a short time they have experienced a phenomenal growth. The movement now is established in
just about every part of the country and in the four years from
1968 through June 1971, some 3,000 have been baptized and
thirty churches have been started. They represent the fastest
growing evangelical group in Spain.

The remainder of the Protestant denominations are relatively small and their history is unknown to me at this time.
The complete recognized listing of these is given on pages 19
and 20 and their size can be noted in relation to the other
denominations and associations. Actually, there are more groups

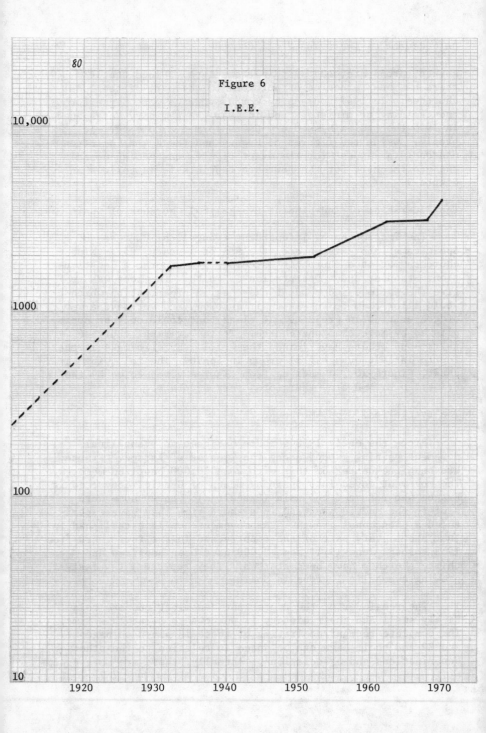

Figure 6

I.E.E.

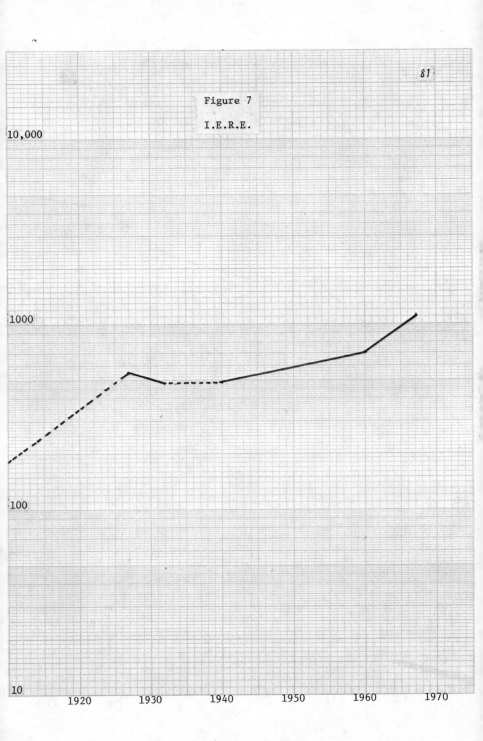

Figure 7

I.E.R.E.

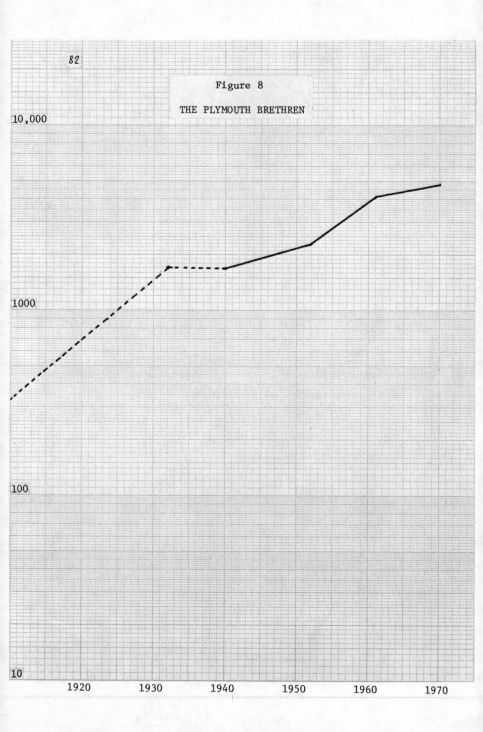

Figure 8

THE PLYMOUTH BRETHREN

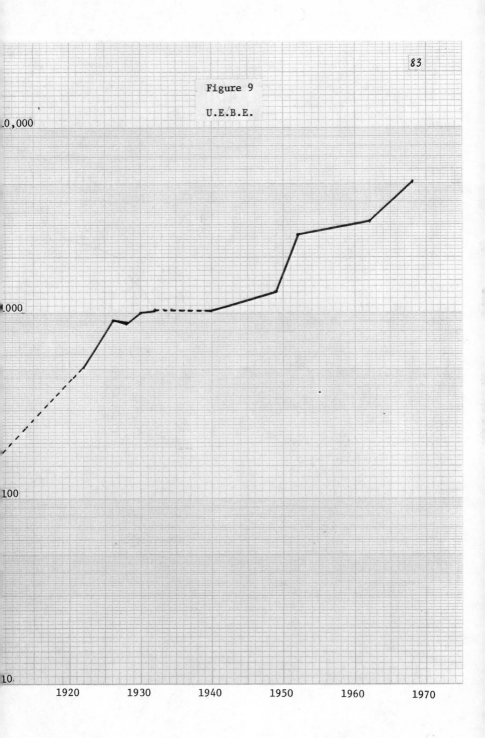

Figure 9

U.E.B.E.

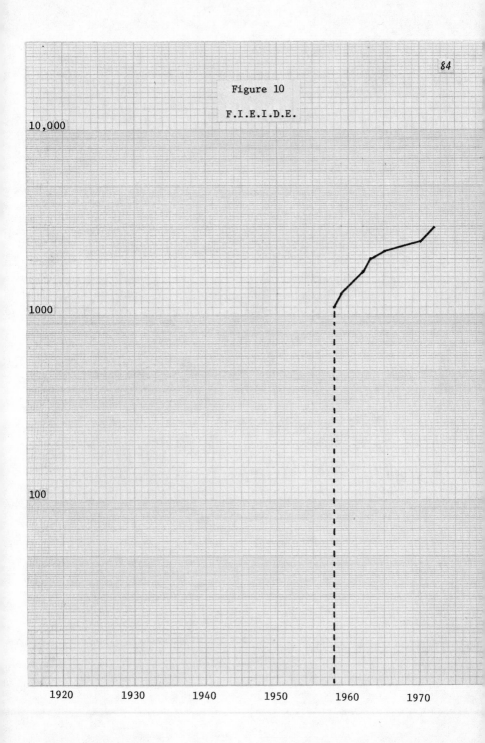

Figure 10

F.I.E.I.D.E.

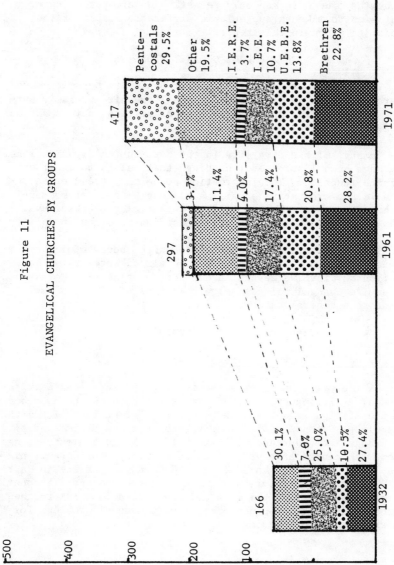

Figure 11

EVANGELICAL CHURCHES BY GROUPS

than are legally recognized at present, but I do not have
access to the information as to their names and sizes. Many
of them have been formed only recently and are not of sufficient size to make an appreciable difference in any of the
statistics given in this report.

PARA-CHURCH ORGANIZATIONS

The para-church organizations of Spain are becoming more
numerous and, in general, they are well organized. Their purposes vary and fill in the many gaps of service that cannot be
carried on by one local church.

Because of the diversity in the para-church organizations,
they have been listed under headings that relate to their pre-
dominate function. The information concerning these organizations is not exhaustive and is meant to give a brief summary
of their purposes. This will give a general picture of what
types and the number of such organizations existing in Spain.

There are certain organizations which, because of their
broader base, do not fit under a specialized category. Their
function may involve several areas and, in general, they serve
the entire evangelical community. The following organizations
are of this general nature.

Organizations of a General Nature

The Evangelical Service of Legal Assistance

Of the para-church organizations, the Evangelical Service
of Legal Assistance is the most important both to the churches
and the mission organizations in Spain. Formed in 1951, as the
Evangelical Defense Commission, for the purpose of representing
the Evangelical Churches of Spain before the government, it has
become the center of a great deal of activity. All questions
of a legal nature are handled in José Cardona's office in Madrid.
He is especially helpful in advising the pastors and missionaries
on matters concerning the laws and their relationships to the
churches. His advice can prevent a multitude of problems for thos
who will ask before acting.

The Spanish Evangelical Alliance

This is an organization which is open to all believers who
affirm the doctrinal statement of the Alliance and who pay the
nominal annual membership fee. It is quite loose in its structure and is mainly devoted to affording a united front in the:
1. fellowship in the Gospel (Philippians 1:5), 2. defense
of the Gospel (Philippians 1:7), and 3. extension of the
Gospel (Philippians 1:12). A committee of advisors, comprised
of some twenty church leaders meet once a year to discuss items
of mutual interest and concern. At the annual meeting an
executive committee is elected as well as a representative to
the European Evangelical Alliance. It is under the auspices
of the Alliance that the Iberian Conference on Evangelism has
been tentatively scheduled for **spring of 1974.**

The Iberian Conference on Evangelism will be an outcome
of the European Congress on Evangelism in Amsterdam in 1971.
The delegates from Spain and Portugal decided that a congress
of this type would be beneficial for the two countries and the
Spanish Evangelical Alliance was asked to be responsible for
it. The conference will have a threefold purpose: 1. To
present a clear testimony of who Evangelical Christians are
and what they believe. 2. To study all of the possible means
of communication to carry the Evangelical message to all of
the Spanish and Portuguese people. 3. To do everything possible that the results of the "Congress" (in Amsterdam), the
best and most effective fruit, be established by means of fra-
ternal colaboration that will perpetuate the animated spirit of
that meeting, contributing a better testimony, and a better
work, for the evangelization of the Iberian Peninsula.

The *alianza* has also been the organization responsible for
the preparation of the Universal Week of Prayer programs in
Spain.

Evangelism in Action

This is an organization which has been founded since the
Law of Religious Liberty and is one hundred per cent for evangelism. In light of the new law, a group of Evangelical leaders
met to discuss the possibilities of new and better methods of
evangelism to be used in all of Spain. The result was the
formation of Evangelism in Action, a Barcelona-based effort.

It is interdenominational in scope and is willing to help
local churches requesting their service. In October 1968, they
sent out a letter explaining who they were, their purposes.
Since that time they have been extremely busy in a variety of
projects which have reached the entire country. They have had
many articles printed in magazines and papers, had a radio
broadcast when the government permitted, and have made extensive use of films. They have many ambitious plans for the
future and a good track record to date.

The Spanish Evangelical Council

Originally an organization composed of representatives of
the major evangelical churches of Spain, the Council gave the
various groups an opportunity to exchange information and a
place to discuss mutual problems. It has a biannual meeting,
usually in May, and representatives of other European countries
are usually present. In recent years the more conservative
groups have withdrawn their support and presence from the
Council and it is no longer the voice of the Spanish Protestants that it used to be. A recent example of this was the
cancellation of the proposed III National Conference of Ministers of the Gospel in Spain under the sponsorship of the Council.
It had to be cancelled at the last moment because of the lack
of support by the major groups. The conference was later held
in Madrid, but under the sponsorship of another group.

Spanish Association of the Evangelical Press and Publications

In May of 1971 the *Asociación de Escritores y Periodistas
Evangélicos* changed their name to the *Asociación Española de
Prensa y Publicaciones Evangélicas*. The possibilities of
having such an association is a sign of the new age in Spain.
Up until recent years only one Evangelical was allowed to have
a press card. That was José Cardona, Secretary of the Evangelical Service of Legal Assistance. Now there are several recognized men from the Evangelicals that have such cards and are
granted the privileges of the press. This organization has
interest in advancing quality publications and using the jour-
nalistic abilities of the Evangelical community for the good
of all. The quality of the work of these men is recognized not
only in Spain, but in all of the Spanish-speaking world.

Literature Ministries

There are in Spain some outstanding publication facilities and the quality and quantity of the literature is far out of proportion to the size of the Evangelical community. To facilitate the listing of these various ministries, I have broken them into four categories: Periodicals, Printers, Bookstores, and Correspondence Courses.

Periodicals

The periodicals printed in Spain for the Evangelical community are not as numerous as one might think or hope. There are only about four that have a very large distribution, but the quality is good. The strict laws concerning the publication of materials for public distribution has doubtless kept several groups from trying to put out a regular publication. The chart on pages 92-93 gives the picture of the periodicals through the years. It lists only those that have a publishing history of more than three consecutive years. At the present time there are a few more in circulation that did not qualify for the chart.

Andalucía Evangélica is the organ of the Southern Association of Evangelical Ministers. It is published occasionally and is done in Algeciras.

Boletín Anual is the official organ of the *Alianza Evangélica Española.*

Carta Abierta Para Usted - A publication of Mario Cignoni Penella which is sent out when funds permit.

Circular del Centro Ecumenico - A monthly bulletin published by the Ecumenical Center of Barcelona.

Edificación Cristiana is a publication of the Plymouth Brethren printed in Madrid.

El Noticiero Evangélico is an unregistered publication of the Darby Brethren.

Juventud - Fe Y Acción - A quarterly publication of the Spanish National Union of Baptist Young People.

La Voz Fundamentalista is a publication of the *Comunión Bautista Independiente* and is another unregistered magazine.

Primera Luz is now being published in conjunction with *Restauración* and is a children's magaaine.

Vida Cristiana is edited by the Darby Brethren and is published at varying intervals.

The following publications also exist, but I am not sure of their affiliation: *Mensajes del Amor* and *Selecciones Cristianas*.

There are youth oriented magazines that come out from time to time, usually the work of some church's youth group, but none have a wide circulation. There may be a few other publications of a local nature that I am not familiar with, but they have yet to become definitely established. There are a few publications sent into the country to individuals and churches from Latin American and the United States. Among the best known are: *La Estrella de la Mañana* from Venezuela, *Certeza* and *Pensamiento Cristiano* from Argentina, and *Decisión* from the United States.

Printers

Comité de Literatura para las Iglesias is the name of the organization headed up by Samuel Vila in Tarrasa. He does a great deal of printing for the various organizations in Spain and Latin America.

Ediciones Alturas S.A.E. is the independent publishing concern of various members of the Plymouth Brethren in Barcelona.

Ediciones Evangélicas Europeas is a Barcelona-based group headed up by José Grau.

Editorial Irmayol is the organization of Juan A. Monroy of the Church of Christ and is located in Madrid.

Publicaciones Portavoz Evangélico is the publishing arm of Worldwide European Fellowship and is headed by Herold Kregel.

Fundació Bíblica is located in Barcelona also and is dedicated to the printing and distribution of evangelical literature in the Catalan language.

Literatura Bíblica is the publication department of the Plymouth Brethren and is located in Madrid.

Juan Bautista de Publicaciones is the Southern Baptist publishing department in Spain.

Mensajes del Amor de Dios is the name of the published work of Pablo Enrique Lemore of the Darby group.

Asociación Cultural de Estudios de La Literatura Reformada

Servicio Editorial de la I.E.E.

In addition to the publishing of materials in Spain, there is a great deal of printed material imported from other countries. Two groups, at least, are dedicated to the importation and distribution of evangelical materials. They are: *Centro de Literatura Cristiana* (Madrid), and the *Centro de Literatura para las Iglesias Evangélicas* (Tarragona). Two of the publishing companies that send in a good bit of material are: *Editorial Caribe* and *Editorial La Aurora*.

Bookstores

When Harold Kregel opened the *Librería Evangélica* in Barcelona in 1965, it was the first of the few evangelical bookstores to open in Spain. It seems that almost every church has its little selection of books for sale and in the major cities evangelical bookstores are now appearing. It is safe to say that acquiring Christian literature is not a problem for the average church member.

The best known bookstores are:

Barcelona:

   Librería Evangélica - Harold Kregel's bookstore.
                        Camelias 19
   Librería Bautista - The Southern Baptist bookstore,
                        Arimón 22.

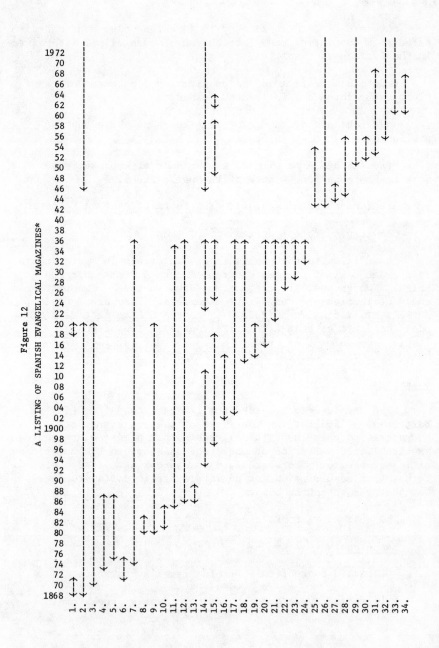

Figure 12

A LISTING OF SPANISH EVANGELICAL MAGAZINES*

*Only magazines published for three years or more are included.
+La Luz, El Cristiano, Revista Cristiana, and El Atalaya combined to become España Evangélica.

#	Title	Years Published	Founded By
1.	El Cristianismo	1869-71 1919	Juan Bautista Cabrera
2.	La Luz	1869-1919 1946-	Antonio Carrasco
3.	El Cristiano	1870-1919	Tract Society
4.	La Aurora de la Gracia	1873-1887	J. Lawrence
5.	La Estrella de la Gracia	1875-1887	J. Lawrence
6.	La Bandera de la Reforma	1871-1875	Pedro Sala
7.	El Amigo de la Infancia	1874-1936	F. Fliedner
8.	El Mensajero de la Salvación	1880-1883	Federico Jowes
9.	Revista Cristiana	1880-1919	F. Fliedner
10.	El Mensajero Cristiano	1881-1884	
11.	El Evangelista	1884-1935	Lund / Payne
12.	El Heraldo	1886-1936	López Rodrieguez
13.	El Atalaya	1886-1889	F. Albricias
14.	El Eco de la Verdad	1893-1910 1923-36 1946-Present	
15.	Esfuerzo Cristiano	1897-1917 1925-36 1949-58 1962-64	Esfuerzo Cristiano
16.	Hojas Dominicales	1901-1914	Uhr / Mateu
17.	El Mensajero de la Verdad	1902-1936	Evangelical Church Mission
18.	Revista Homilética	1913-1936	E. Lund
19.	La Biblia	1914-1919	Spanish Society of Tracts & Books
20.	La Aurora de Galicia	1916-1936	Brethren (Plymouth)
+21.	España Evangélica	1920-1936	I.E.E. / I.E.R.E.
22.	La Buena Nueva	1927-1936	Bible Society
23.	El Joven Cristiano	1929-1936	Brethren (Plymouth)
24.	Verdades	1931-1936	Southern Baptist
25.	Constancia	1943-1953	Independent
26.	Carta Circular	1943-Present	I.E.E.
27.	Escudriñador Bíblico	1944-1947	Brethren (Plymouth)
28.	El Camino	1945-1955	Brethren (Plymouth)
29.	Nuestra Labor	1951-Present	Southern Baptist
30.	El Cristiano Español	1952-1955	Evangelical Christian Mission
31.	La Voz Juvenil	1953-1970	Southern Baptist
32.	Restauración	1955-Present	A. Monroy
33.	Portavoz Evangélico	1959-Present	José Grau and Herold Kregel
34.	Testimonio Evangélico	1961-1969	F.I.E.I.D.E. (Fernández 1972)

Madrid:

Librería Bíblica Española - The mission Acción Biblique
                    Fernández de los Ríos 91
Librería de Blanco - Owned by Ramón Blanco
                    Pelicano 26
Librería Evangélicos - Run by Irma Fliedner
                    Calatrava 34
Librería Cristiana - Juan Monroy of the Church of Christ
                    Flor Alta 2
Literatura Bíblica - The Brethren
                    Trafalgar 32, 2°A
Centro Literatura Cristiano - Christian Literature
                    Crusade, José Antonio 66, 7°,12
Sociedad Bíblica - Bible Society
                    Joaquin García Morato 133

Seville:

La Semilla Preciosa - Missionary Soul Winning Fellowship
                    Ramón y Cajal Bl. 10

Málaga:

Librería Bíblica - Global Outreach Mission
                    Pasaje Aranzazu 9

Valencia:

It is my understanding that the Christian Literature
Crusade has opened a new store here, it is located at Cuba 31.

Correspondence Courses

One of the most widely used methods of instruction in the
Evangelical faith is the correspondence course. There are
several large centers with almost every denomination and group
sending out a course of some type. Most are of the "Light of
Life" type on the Gospel of John, but some groups have become
involved in series of courses designed not only to reach, but
also to teach new believers. Again, it would be impossible to
name all of the various groups participating in this type of
ministry. The number of enrolled students in these courses
would number several thousand. In some areas of the country

the concern of the Catholic Church over the number of people
taking courses from the Evangelicals has prompted the Catholic Church to develop a series of correspondence courses of
their own. One such course is a very strong attack on the Protestants. It is made up of sixteen lessons and is published by
Fe Católica. Most of their courses, however, are designed to
strengthen Catholics in the doctrines of their faith.

Theological Training Institutions

At present there are nine evangelical training institutions
in Spain. None of them is very large and in general they constitute the system of training normal to that received by those
that head up the program. Without any evaluation of the
schools, they are as follows:

Centro Evangélico de Estudios Bíblicos

An interdenominational effort in Barcelona under the sponsorship of the Spanish Evangelical Alliance. It is a night
school and probably has the largest enrollment of any present
program. Most of the leading pastors and laymen of the Barcelona area cooperate in this effort as well as one or two
missionaries.

Cursos de Estudios Bíblicos

This is under the direction of the Plymouth Brethren and
has its center in Madrid. Much of the training is done by way
of correspondence courses and in short term, intensive Bible
courses of about a month's duration at the center in Madrid.

Escuela Bíblica Bethel

This is an interdenominational training school for girls
run by the Bible Club Movement near Segovia (La Granja).
Maria Bolet has been able to bring this back to Spain after
several years in the Pyrenees just across the French border.
In 1972 there were seven girls enrolled in the school.

Escuela de Teología

Under the sponsorship of the Federation of Independent
Evangelical Churches of Spain, the School of Theology has discontinued its residence program and is experimenting with an
extension system. Directed by a missionary, the instructors
travel to various of the Federation churches giving instruction
to interested students on three levels. In 1972 there were some

fifty registered students. There has been some talk of
reopening the resident program again.

Instituto Bíblico Español

This is the Assemblies of God school located in the out-
skirts of Madrid. Although a denominational school, it is
open to students from other churches that care to send young
people to study in its three year program. It is directed by
Terry Gonzales and in 1972 had eight students.

Instituto Bíblico de Málaga

This is an interdenominational school directed by Augustín
Santana in Málaga. It is open to both sexes and in 1972 was
training four students.

Seminario Adventista Español

The denominational school of the Seventh-day Adventists
which is located in Valencia. Directed by a committee of three
men, it trains leaders for its own churches. In 1972 there were
thirty students enrolled.

Seminario Bautista Español

One of the schools which has recently moved to Madrid is
that of the Southern Baptists. Directed by Gerald A. McNeely,
the school meets in the facilities of Emmanuel Baptist Church
and has plans to build in Alcobendas (just outside Madrid).
In 1972 it had an enrollment of four couples and one single
student.

Seminario Evangélico Unido

This school is under the dual sponsorship of the Spanish
Evangelical Church (.I.E.E.) and the Spanish Reformed Episcopal
Church (I.E.R.E.). Under the direction of Daniel Vidal, it
conducts classes from 5:00 to 10:00 p.m. five days a week.
During 1972 there were 17 students enrolled, nine of whom were
preparing for the ministry.

The Greater Europe Mission has plans for the beginning of
a school in the Barcelona area by the Fall of 1974. There are
also plans underway for a training program to be started in
Madrid on the Theological Education by Extension style.

By and large, the schools represent large investments of
time and money for the training of small numbers of students.

They are financed, with few exceptions, by foreign funds. Needless to say, there has to be a better way of training leadership that is within the realm of possibility for the local congregations.

Youth Oriented Ministries

The Evangelical Church in Spain is becoming more aware of
the potential of its youth and the necessity of preserving them
in the church. They are also coming to recognize the need of
the youth of Spain in general being confronted with the truths
of God's Word and that they need to be given the opportunity
to have a life directed from above. This concern has caused
at least three groups to organize and emphasize their work
among the youth of Spain. There are other less formally organized groups among the university students, but in general this
is a neglected area of work.

Juventud para Cristo (Youth for Christ)

Originally formed some years ago, before the passing of
the Law of Religious Liberty, Youth for Christ had to be dis-
banded. Its center of operations was in Barcelona, the most
liberal section of the country as far as religious liberty was
concerned, but apparently it was a bit premature. It has
recently (May 29, 1971) been revived and a new committee formed.
Aimed at the youth of Spain, it was again confined to the
immediate Barcelona area at first. It has since named a director for the area of La Mancha and has plans for other areas as
soon as it is practical. Through youth rallies once a month
and the ministry of special evangelistic teams sent out to
local churches, as well as special emphasis during summer vaca-
tion periods, it is seeking to reach the youth of Spain with
the Gospel.

Grupo Bíblico Universitario

This is a group which apparently is trying to pull together
several groups of Evangelical students at the various universities of Spain. In some of the universities Bible studies have
been started by missionaries, church groups, and even by university students themselves. These were often started independently
of any organization and sometimes there would be several trying
to form groups on a campus at the same time without knowledge
of the otheres. This was especially true at the University of
Madrid at one time. In Barcelona, where the name of GBU

originated, the groups are under the direction of a representative of Inter-Varsity. At the present there are small groups
in Madrid, Barcelona, Valencia and Santiago de Compostela.
They have been able to hold some weekend retreats for the
students at camps and some conferences have been held but the
work still needs more leaders to tie it together. There are
several large universities in Spain where there is no Evangelical
group at all and the work among university students of Spain is
a neglected area in general.

Cruzada Estudiantil y Profesional para Cristo (Campus Crusade for Christ International)

     This organization known all around the world is directed
in Spain by a former Spanish pastor, José Monells. It is
centered in Barcelona and through its Bible study groups in the
university, courses in the local churches, and by evangelistic
teams the work is growing and its influence spreading to other
parts of the country. Towards the end of 1972 the organization
announced the addition of two couples and five single workers
to the staff for assignments in the various faculties of the
University of Barcelona, the University of Madrid, for the
development of their lay program, and for a ministry in music.

Camps and Conference Grounds

     There is a great need in Spain for facilities for camp
programs for the Evangelical christians. Although this has
been recognized in various circles, there has not been the
ability to provide for this need. It is a type program which
is usually beyond the ability of a single church and thus will
have to be undertaken by mission boards or on the denominational
level. The Southern Baptists have the only camp that would be
considered adaquate by state-side standards. It is lamentable
if others are not beginning camps because they feel that they
cannot have all of the facilities needed at the beginning.
Young people have a great capacity for having a good time in
less than ideal conditions and a modest attempt could be added
to year by year.

     The Plymouth Brethren have the largest number of facilities
and these are located in the various areas of Spain where they
have the largest concentration of churches. The following is
a list of the camps that exist a present according to my knowledge:

Agua Dulce - This is a modest house in the mountains near Barcelona. It is the property of the I.E.E. and is suitable for small retreats.

Berea - A Brethren camp about 10 kilometers outside Barcelona at Fontrubi. I am not sure of its size or facilities.

Campamento de Castineriras - A camp located in the area of Galicia in the province of La Coruña. I am not sure of its affiliation but would assume that it is Brethren.

Campamento Esperanza - Located in the province of Guadalajara.

El Sendero de las Uvas - A camp located in Villaescusa, Salamanca.

La Granja - The Bible Club camp located to the north of Madrid. It has a capacity of 30-35.

Mar Cristalina - On the beach just south of Valencia is this camp of the Torchbearers. It is a small piece of land with a house for young peoples retreats. Groups come from various countries to participate and it is open to groups from Spain as well.

Residencia Evangélica Bautista en Denia - This is the well-equipped camp grounds of the Southern Baptists. It is located south of Valencia on the coast at Denia.

Residencia de Verano "Villa Adelfos" - Located in the province of Valencia at Alcoceber.

Vallgorgina - Another camp of the Brethren located about 40 kilometers outside of Barcelona.

Villa - In the Northwest part of Spain above Portugal is another of the small grounds operated by the Brethren.

I believe that there is another camp in the area of Murcia but am not sure. Also I believe that there is a small camp in Asturias, but again am not sure who runs it nor its exact location.

72195

Radio Programs

The broadcasting of Evangelical radio programs within Spain
has been an on again off again proposition. After the Law of
Religious Liberty was passed in 1967 many Evangelicals had hoped
to be able to air radio programs. After some time at least four
programs were started and continued for about three months (July
to September 1970). Some programs were allowed to resume in 1972
for another period of time, a bit longer than the first attempt,
before again being discontinued by the government. At this writing of this study the programs are still not being allowed within the country.

While broadcasting from within the country has not been
permitted with any regularity there have been a number of programs beamed into Spain from Portugal and Monte Carlo. The
response to these programs indicates that a good number of non-
Evangelicals are listening.

Evangelical Schools

The problem of educating their children can be a difficult
one for the Evangelical christian in Spain. There are few
Evangelical schools, the public schools are crowded and run by
the Catholic Church, and the private schools are expensive. The
law does allow the parents to write to the school officials and
have their children exempt from the religious instruction classes
but the social pressures and regular textbooks, which are full
of Catholic doctrine, constantly place the children in difficult
circumstances. Much emphasis is given to the preperation of the
children for their first communion and the child who does not
participate is not looked upon with favor either by the officials
or by their peers.

There needs to be many more schools started for the education of children of non-Catholics. Before the Civil War this
was an important part of the Evangelical Church program. In
1932 there were 116 such schools in Spain. Since the War there
has not been the ability to revive these to any extent and at
present there are only nine such schools being operated. There
need to be many more. The schools are as follows:

Colegio Evangélico (Barcelona)
Colegio Evangélico "Bethel" (Alicante)
Colegio Evangélico "Casa de Paz" (El Escorial)
Colegio Evangélico "El Porvenir" (Madrid)
Colegio Evangélico "Juan de Valdes" (Madrid)

Colegio Evangélico "Maranatha" (Algeciras)
Colegio Evangélico (Sabadell) (This has now been closed.)
Colegio Evangélico "San Juan" (Tarrasa)
Escuela Evangélica "La Esperanza" (Alicante)

Social Concern Ministries

Although their resources are not great, the Spanish
Evangelical Christians attempt to care for their own. They
have established homes for the aged and homes for infants and
have an Evangelical Hospital in Barcelona. These are modest
attempts in some ways but they do demonstrate the genuine
desire of the Evangelicals to serve. At present there are
seven homes for the aged and they are located in: Lineares,
Madrid, Mataro, Reus, two in Sta. Coloma de Gramanet, and the
last in Villafranca del Panades. The five children's homes
are located in: Barcelona, El Escorial, Sta. María (Mallorca)
and two are in Madrid.

THE CULTS

Another of the unfortunate circumstances in Spain is the
failure of the Catholic Church to make a distinction between
the Evangelical Church and the Cults. They refer to both as
"Protestants." In his book *Diálogo con Protestantes*, Luis E.
Bravo tries to give Catholics counsel on how to deal with the
Protestants. One of his most serious mistakes is that he sees
no difference between a Baptist, for example, and a Jehovah's
Witness. This distinction just is not felt to exist and it
greatly complicates the situation of Catholic/Evangelical
relationships.

Jehovah's Witnesses

The largest group of the cults to be considered is the
Jehovah's Witnesses. They are literally everywhere. I continually had to explain to people that I was not a Jehovah's
Witness in my visitation and it was not uncommon to see them
traveling in pairs down the streets of a village. Although
they have been one of the last groups to receive legal recognition by the government, they have the largest following
of all non-Catholic organizations according to their figures.
In 1950 they reported having only 93 members in Spain. In 1970
they reported, in their yearbook, a membership of 10,086
scattered in 112 congregations. That is almost twice the size

of any Evangelical group in Spain at present as far as membership is concerned.

The Jehovah's Witnesses have had a special appeal among the numerous anti-clerical Catholics. Their message is negative, and their zeal is outstanding. Armed with a supply of books they are out visiting door to door in every city and village. These teams try to sell their literature and interest the people in having a Bible study conducted in their home. If a person is willing to have a study a teacher is sent to conduct this on a weekly basis. Those who have really been interested in a Bible study have often been disappointed to find that the Bible is not really the textbook. They are given studies from books which teach a system of doctrine particular to the Jehovah's Witnesses and backed up by a special translation of the Scriptures. Once indoctrinated the person is armed with verses to prove that the Jehovah's Witness faith is the true one and paired with another person to go visiting door to door. The activities of the group are very simular from country to country.

Very often a person is not lost to the Gospel simply because of his experience with a *Testigo de Jehová* Bible study. This may become the first step toward a true experience with Christ. I have personally met many who at one time or another were associated with a Jehovah's Witness Bible study but stopped because they could not accept the teaching. It is especially difficult for the normal Spaniard to turn against his family and country and yet this is what many people seem to feel is required. These "drop-outs" are often open to know what the Bible really teaches and often find their way into an Evangelical church.

The rapid expansion of the Witnesses has caused concern among both the Catholics and the Evangelicals. Both have been busy preparing materials informing their members of the errors in doctrine as well as their methods of operation. The Witnesses have come under considerable criticism for their stand on blood transfusions and their refusal to serve in the military services. The latter in Spain is a serious affair, almost equal to treason. The law makes no provision for a consciensious objector and refusal to serve in the military brings a sentence of six years and a day in prison. Upon release from prison the person will be asked to serve in the military again and a refusal brings another sentence of six

years and a day. This could conceivably continue for life.
The government is looking into the injustice of this law but
is having trouble as it falls under military rather than civil
jurisdiction. In spite of this hardship, in 1970 there were
182 young men serving their time in prison for objecting to
serve their country because of their religious convictions.
Of these 180 were Jehovah's Witnesses.

Mormons

In recent years the Mormons have also gone into Spain.
The first convert was a lawyer in Madrid. He has now become
the head of their work and has his office near the University
of Madrid. I have not been able to obtain the exact figures
for this movement, and they have not been overly anxious to
let people know how they are doing. I do know that at one
time they had 30 of their young two year missionaries from the
United States working in the country. The work started in
1962, I believe, and by 1971 it had 11 churches or meeting
places legalized by the government. I had occasion to meet
two of their workers one day but other than that have not
had any experience with them in Spain, nor have I met a
Spaniard who was influenced by their teachings.

Seventh-day Adventist

I have included the Seventh-day Adventists in the category
of a cult as this is the way they are normally listed by the
Evangelicals in Spain. Their progress in Spain has not been
spectacular, but it has been steady. I was able to obtain the
information on their growth directly from their records and it
is charted in figure No. 14 from 1935 through 1971. I chose
1935 as the place to start because it was the year prior to the
Civil War and gives a good basis for comparison through those
difficult years. In 1935 there were 10 churches and 358 members.
At the end of the War they had grown by 45 members and still
listed 10 churches. By 1945 the membership had slipped to 296.
The next five years brought something of a recovery and in 1950
the membership was 635 in the 10 churches. Between 1950 and
1955 they were able to start 5 new churches and the membership
increased to 912. Two more churches were added by 1960 and the
membership climbed to 1,336. From 1960 to 1965 there was an
increase of five more churches and 5 ordained pastors and the
membership was up to 1,964. In 1971 there were 34 churches and
2,974 members.

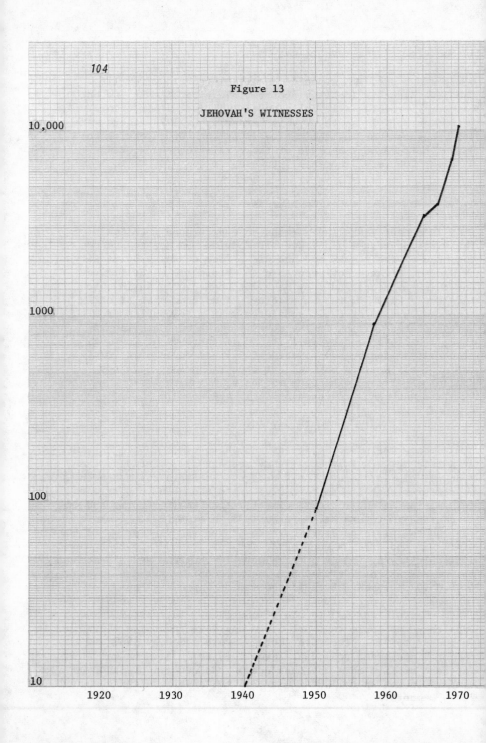

Figure 13

JEHOVAH'S WITNESSES

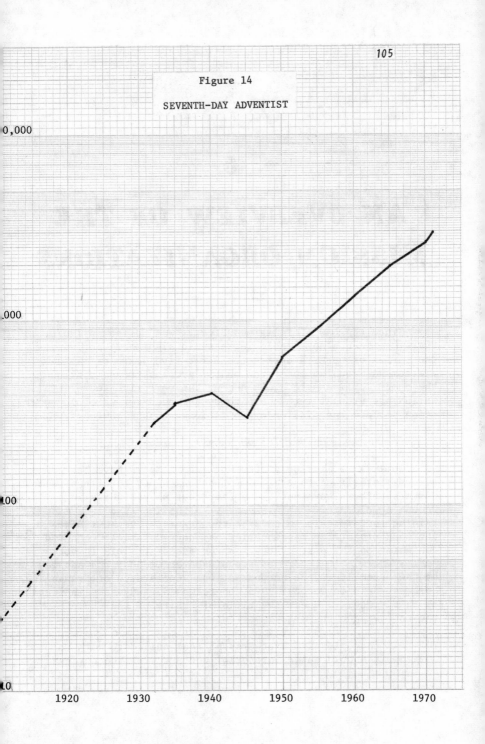

Figure 14

SEVENTH-DAY ADVENTIST

6

AN OVERVIEW OF THE MISSION ORGANIZATIONS

Since the Law of Religious Liberty was passed in 1967, there has been a noticeable increase in missionary activity. The influx of workers during the first five years of the new freedom has doubled the force and if present trends continue, the number will double again during the next five years. This influx has brought into sharp focus the need for careful cooperation between the mission organizations and the churches.

CHURCH/MISSION RELATIONSHIPS

While some mission groups working in Spain have been conscious of the fact that care must be taken not to offend fellow workers, others have not. The fact that no one works in a vacuum should alert the missionary to the importance of maintaining good relationships with the Spanish churches. The increase of foreign missionaries has caused some concern and confusion on the part of the Spanish pastors. This is not entirely new. In the conclusions and recommendations adopted by the assembly of the Second National Conference of Evangelical Workers, held in October 1965, there was already some indication of this concern. Under the title of "Unity of the Churches," the following clause was inserted:

All those foreign brothers who feel called to work in Spain should enter into prior contact with the national

churches and associations to obtain a better cohesion
in our evangelical labor (Poveda 1965:50).

Unfortunately, this has not been practical as new mission groups
have not known who to contact. There is not any one organization that speaks for all of the Evangelical community, especially in such an important issue. The most important single
organization to contact is the Evangelical Service of Legal
Assistance (formerly the Evangelical Defense Commission). The
next most important organization would probably be the Foreign
Mission Consultation Committee.

Foreign Missions Consultation Committee

This organization was formed at the request of some national
pastors to help bridge the gap between the mission agencies and
the national churches. It is a voluntary organization, with no
legislative capacity, which is open to all mission groups, denominational or independent. The sole purpose of E.F.M.C.C. is to
pass on the information which has been voluntarily supplied by
the missionaries and mission agencies.

Through a yearly questionnaire the E.F.M.C.C. keeps up to
date on the participating missions concerning the number of
workers, their names, and areas of work. There is also a record
of the main objectives of a given group in Spain and other
miscellaneous information. By means of this central source of
information a national pastor can obtain information about a
mission agency, a missionary, and their work. No judgments are
made as to the merits of the mission or missionary and only
submitted information is passed on. As of June 1971, there
were nineteen missions cooperating in the E.F.M.C.C.

MISSION AGENCIES

One convenient way to survey the mission organizations
presently in Spain is to divide them into three groups. The
first group is constituted by the European Boards, the second
by the Third World Missions, and the third by the North American Boards. Under the last group there will be a need to make
some distinctions between church-planting groups and service
agencies. This distinction is not always clearly defined since
the "service agencies" are often helping in church planting and
the agencies considering themselves as church-planting groups
also have ministries that are not directly involved in church

planting. It should be noted here that in Spain there have not
been the diversity of ministries common to other countries.
This has been the result of legal and circumstancial restric-
tions. Thus, we do not have the great amounts of energy invested
in medical and education institutions that characterize the
missionary enterprise of so many areas of the world.

European Boards

Some of the oldest works in Spain are those of European
Missionary societies. The proximity of their home offices has
given them opportunity to know the needs and respond as concerned neighbors. One of the oldest and better known is the
Bible Society.

The British and Foreign Bible Society

The interest of this organization dates back to 1805 when
there was a concern expressed for the Spanish prisoners of war
in England. In 1808 these prisoners were given New Testaments
upon sailing for Spain. Beyond this, nothing was done until
1821 when it formed a correspondence committee in Gibraltar.
Through this, a few thousand copies of the Scriptures entered
Spain. It was not until 1835 that workers were actually able
to enter Spain itself. The best known of these was George
Borrows. His travels through Spain for five years are recorded
in the now classic work of his *The Bible in Spain*. The other
worker who is not mentioned very often was Lt. Graydon. Although not officially a member of the Bible Society, he travel-
led along the southern coast of Spain and up to Barcelona. Both
he and Borrows were encouraged at the response of the people
and were disappointed when forced to leave the country in 1837.

The work of the Society was then a bit sporadic for the
next few years. In 1847 Dr. James Thomson visited Spain, but
could do very little. Seven years later the Society sent a
packet of 950 Bibles, Testaments, and portions to a man in
southern Spain for distribution, but it was not until the
1900's that colporteurs were able to be used. Between 1905
and 1919 the Society had an average of 20 colporteurs working
in Spain. They were able to continue the work through World
War I and in 1920 has 19 colporteurs. They averaged 140,000
copies of the Scriptures distributed per year and in 1935
reached the total of 305,000 copies distributed. The Society

was greatly encouraged in its work and had just entered into a two year plan of advance with a Bible van called "The George Borrow Bible Van" when the Spanish Civil War began. The Society was immediately put under the protection of the British Embassy and continued a curtailed ministry through the war. At the end of 1937, there were nine staff members scattered across the country and the Bible Van had been requisitioned by the government for use as an ambulance. The ten years following the war (1939-1949) were characterized by a cautious and defensive policy (Roe 1965:281-5). On August 7, 1940, the Spanish government confiscated all of the Bible Society's stock of Bibles and orders were given to take examples of their publications wherever and whenever they were found. From 1940 until 1963 the work was carried on in a precarious manner, always in danger of having its stock confiscated and being denounced to government authorities.

With the change of government policy in the early part of 1963 came an authorization for the Society to resume operations. A special inauguration service for the new offices of the Bible Society was held in December of that year by the English Ambassador (Flores 1969:12-13). Since that time the name of the Society has been changed to the *Asociación Bíblica Española*, helping to avoid the impression that the Society is a foreign enterprise. I have included it here mainly for convenience and because of its historical background.

Action Biblique

This is a Swiss group which has been working in Spain for only a couple of years. Its present representatives are two brothers who have opened a modern bookstore in Madrid. The plans of the group include the operation of a correspondence course center and the expectation of being involved in evangelistic endeavors in the future.

Ambassadors for Christ International

This was originally an Australian mission group now centered in England that began work in Spain in 1948. It is mainly involved in literature distribution at fairs and in the villages by use of a book van and teams of workers. At present it supports two Spanish couples.

Assemblies of God (Great Britain and Ireland)

I am not well informed on this group, but it seems to be represented at present by two couples in the areas of Aguilas (Murcia) on the south coast of Spain. In 1970 the work was comprised of three churches and three groups with a total of 35 baptized believers.

The Brethren (Plymouth)

One of the oldest works in Spain and the one with the greatest visible results would be that of the Brethren. Two missionaries, W. Gould and G. Lawrence, arrived in 1863 to begin the work, but were unable to do much until the revolution of 1868. They were joined by Mr. H. Payne in 1868 and the work was centered around Barcelona and Madrid. Their most extensive work has traditionally been in the northern section of the country called Galicia.

In the earlier stages of the work there was a good deal of colportage work and visitation. The Civil War also caused the Brethren some setbacks, but they have made good progress since. Some of the first missionaries back into the country were Brethren and they have been good workers. The most notable was the late Mr. Ernest Trenchard. His writing and teaching abilities have done much in helping to train the leadership of the Assemblies all over Spain. At present there are four foreign couples working in the country.

Capernwray Missionary Fellowship of Torchbearers

A British-based youth program that has a couple living just outside of Valencia. The work is camp for young people, right on the Mediterranean and has groups from various countries of Europe.

Child Evangelism Fellowship (British Branch)

Centered just outside of Barcelona, the work is comprised of one couple from Ireland and a couple of Spanish ladies. They help in the area of children's work, teaching DVBS type programs in various churches.

Deutsche Missionsgemeinschaft

This is a German group about which I have no information.

European Christian Mission

This is a British group that supports a single lady in the Barcelona area. She is involved in teaching in a local church situation and has published a series of Sunday School lessons.

European Missionary Fellowship

The work of this mission is presently comprised of supporting national pastors and aiding existing churches in various parts of Spain. I believe that they have only one single lady actually in Spain at present.

Evangelical European Mission

This is a Swiss group that has been working in Spain since 1958. It is involved in Literature to a great extent and supports a good number of leading pastors.

International Miners Mission

This is a group formed in 1906 to make known the saving truths of the Gospel to miners, metal workers, and their families in England and abroad. Their work in Spain has been very limited and at present consists of a Spanish couple working in La Mancha.

Misión Evangélica para España

This was a mission organization from Holland which worked in literature distribution for evangelism. It was mainly centered in La Linea and I am not sure if it is still functioning in Spain.

Misión Francesa del Alto Aragón

This was a group which was helping support various Spanish pastors in the section of Spain which borders France. It had offices in France and Switzerland and I am not sure if it is still aiding pastors in Spain or if the work has been discontinued.

New Testament Missionary Union

This work is carried on in three areas of Spain and has
been carried on since before the Civil War. Although the information I have received indicated that they have several groups,
there are no records available. They do have a correspondence
course ministry and employ New Testament church methods. They
tend to be a rather closed group. At present there are eight
workers in Spain.

Salvation Army

It is my understanding that one couple has moved into
the area of Galicia to begin a work. It is still too soon to
know much about their efforts.

The Spanish Evangelical Mission

This is a Dutch group that has helped in financing the
education of Spanish young people for the ministry.

Spanish Gospel Mission

The first missionary of the board was Rev. Percy Buffard.
He first became interested in Spain while teaching English in
Santander in 1907. In 1913 the mission was formed and in 1915
Mr. Buffard married and he and his bride settled in Castellon.
Two years later they moved to Valdepeñas. During the Second
Republic the work was moving forward and they had 16 churches in
the area of La Mancha. In July of 1936 the Civil War began and
the missionaries were forced to leave. In 1943 an orphanage was
started by Irene Perez. It was at first begun to house the
children of Evangelical Pastors executed as a result of the war
and to keep the children from having to be put into Catholic
institutions. It was closed in 1950 by the Spanish authorities.

The Ernest Browns arrived in 1946 and permission was given
to reopen the churches. In 1947 Bible Courses were begun in
the mission house to train Spanish pastors. In 1953 it was
divided into two sections, one for boys and one for girls. This
ministry has since been discontinued and there are no foreign
missionaries with this group presently in Spain. The mission
does continue to support a number of Spanish pastors (Brown
1964). In 1970 the work consisted of 9 churches, 8 other groups,
and 276 baptized believers.

Swiss Record Mission

This group has been using correspondence courses and distributing records in Spain. It is represented by a single lady and I have no details as to the number enrolled in their course.

Third World Missions

Although I only have knowledge of one group at present that is a Third World Mission, I expect that in the future this will be one area of increased activities. I personally had letters from three other groups while in Spain asking about the conditions and possibilities of Latin Americans working in Spain. This is something new to many people as Latin America has been and is still considered a mission field in its own right. However, if we expect our work to be considered Biblical, we must not only be expecting to see third world missionaries in Spain, but Spanish missionaries being sent out to other areas of the world. Recent research has revealed that there are over two hundred third world mission organizations at present. There are probably many more unknown to us, as well as others which are being formed every day.

Misión Evangélica para España

I believe this is an Argentina-based group with some two couples and a single lady presently in Spain. It is of Pentecostal background.

North American Groups (Church Planting)

By far the largest number of missionaries in Spain at present are the representatives of North American agencies. It is difficult to write much about them as many are relatively new in Spain. The main item of interest in this is the sign of maturity on the part of some of these boards. Instead of beginning their work with newly appointed candidates, they have pulled in experienced workers from their Latin American fields in many instances. These proven workers give solidity to the work and decrease the possibilities of harmful mistakes in the important steps of beginning a new work. I expect that in the next five years there will be a tremendous increase in new missionaries and new churches established in Spain.

The mission agencies are broken into two areas, and we
will begin with the groups that are considered as having a church
planting emphasis.

Assemblies of God

The Assemblies have had a work in Spain for many years.
They have not restricted their efforts to any one area and until
recently have not been particularly successful. Since 1968
they have had a large number of new missionaries come into the
country and have branched out in their ministries. In 1969
they began with the correspondence course program. In the same
year they also began the Bible Institute in Ronda. It has
since been moved to Madrid. They experimented with a Coffee
Bar ministry on the coast near Barcelona and have also used a
radio ministry program for the publicizing of the Correspondence
Courses, both in Spain and Portugal. The broadcasts are from a
station in Portugal and use tapes of Hermano Pablo. The last
count I had, they had 19 missionaries in Spain.

Association of Baptists for World Evangelism

This is another new group to Spain. It is working in cooperation with other groups of similar persuasion and has a
strong emphasis on evangelism. At present I believe that there
are three couples representing this group.

Baptist International Mission

This is a work that has been started in the Madrid area in
the mid 60's. Recently it has received a number of new workers
and it colaborates with several groups in the *Comunión Bautista
Independiente*. I believe that they have four couples now on
the field.

Bible Baptist Fellowship

A new group to Spain with one couple and working with
Baptist International Missions.

Bible Christian Union, Inc.

I have no information on the number of missionaries and the
areas of their work. I believe it consists of a couple of single
women in the area around Malaga.

Bible Club Movement

This was first introduced in Spain in 1933 with the arrival
of Maria Bolet. She was forced to leave Spain for many years
and only returned since the new law of religious liberty has
been in effect. There is a Bible School for girls located in
La Granja and there are two other foreign workers as well as a
number of Spanish ladies associated with the work.

Canary Island Gospel Mission

This is a small group that has had a work in the Canary
Islands for some time. It has only recently become known by
its present name. It is composed of two couples and will probably not be continued after their departure from the field.

Central American Mission

One of the newest and most active of the mission agencies
in Spain. A team of five couples was pulled from the Latin
American scene and a carefully planned entrance was made into
Spain in 1971. The first couple moved into the Barcelona area
to work with their Sunday School materials and teacher training
programs. Since then the rest of the team has arrived to begin
church planting and evangelistic ministries. I believe that
they have five couples in Spain at the present time.

Free Will Baptist

Although at present there is no worker with the Free Will
Baptists in Spain, they will soon be sinding in a couple.

Global Outreach, Inc. (Formerly European Evangelistic Crusade)

Working in the Malaga area of Spain, they as yet have no
churches and operate a bookstore. At present they have two
couples in Spain and also support some national workers.

Gospel Missionary Union

This is a group that is located in Spain, but is not
actually working with Spanish-speaking people. Forced out of
North Africa, three couples set up their printing and correspondence course ministry in Malaga and continue the work in
North Africa.

Greater Europe Mission

Although the mission has had workers in Spain for some time, now the present missionaries have all arrived within the last ten years. At present it has no established churches and is planning to open a Bible Institute in the Barcelona area about the fall of 1974. At present there are three couples and one single lady representing the work there.

Missionary and Soul Winning Fellowship (Cristianos en Acción)

This is a group working in Santander. A team effort is conducted with one couple and two single ladies. In 1970 the work comprised one established church of about 15 members. They have had a rather large turnover of people in their area.

Open Bible Standard Mission

Another of the new groups to enter Spain, the Open Bible Standard Mission, has quickly adapted to the new work. It is represented by a couple who worked in Cuba for five years prior to going to Spain in 1971 and has one church established in Barcelona. It also helps support a Cuban pastor living in Madrid and forming a church there.

Oriental Missionary Society

Another of the groups turning to Spain as a new field. They plan to send two couples from their work in Colombia and have one couple preparing in the United States at present. They have one national pastor in Spain.

Southern Baptist Convention (Foreign Mission Board)

The largest of the foreign mission agencies and one of the oldest to have a work in Spain. It has all the ministries characteristic of this mission in other countries and the second largest number of established churches in Spain. Only the Brethren have more. Recently they moved their seminary from Barcelona to Madrid and continue an active program of evangelism. The last count that I have of this agency indicated 28 missionaries in the country.

Spanish Evangelical Educational Crusade

Represented by one couple in the Barcelona area, they have ᴜevoted their time to the training of young people, especially in the area of secondary schooling.

The Evangelical Alliance Mission

In 1952 the first couple for TEAM was accepted for work in Spain. They had been working in Archena for some years and now associated with the mission. Soon afterward they were forced to leave the country where they started a work with the Spanish immigrants in France. The next effort was in 1954 when a couple unable to go back into Portugal moved to Madrid to work. Closely related to the Brethren in the early days, they now have a Correspondence course ministry, one established church, and three groups in formation. At one time they operated the Madrid Bible Institute (from 1962-1969). At present they have five couples and one single lady in Spain.

United Presbyterian Church, USA

At the present time there is one couple working with the United Presbyterian Church in Spain. He is a professor at the seminary in Madrid and also pastors the English-speaking Madrid Community Church.

United World Mission

A group that has been instrumental in working in difficult areas. It is represented by one American couple and an American lady who first went to Cuba to work. There she met and married a Spanish fellow. They have returned to Spain to serve the Lord and have been used in starting new churches and training young men for the work. Their daughter and son-in-law are now with the work also.

West Indies Mission

One of the latest groups to start in Spain, it now has one couple from the states and a Cuban couple in the Madrid area. Actually, there has been one of their Cuban workers in the Canary Islands for some time, but it is just since 1972 that they have officially worked as a mission in Spain.

World Baptist Fellowship

One of the groups working with the *Comunión Bautista Independiente*. I am not familiar with their work and believe that they have three couples in Spain.

Worldwide Evangelization Crusade

A group which has just recently begun to move forward. That, I suppose, is due to the fact that with the new religious liberty they have had more new workers. Up until around 1970 there was only a single lady working in the Canary Islands. There are now two more couples. They have one established church in Madrid.

Worldwide European Fellowship

Working in the Barcelona area, this work is known mainly by the work of Harold Kregel. He is one of the missionaries to have served in Spain during the hard years and is probably the best known and most respected foreign workers in Spain. Involved in many evangelistic enterprizes and operator of a bookstore in Barcelona, Harold cooperates with almost all works and is sought out for advice and counsel by missionaries and nationals alike. At present the work is comprised of some four single ladies and two couples.

Independent Missionaries

This is the hardest group to keep track of. It is impossible to be exact on the number of independent missionaries working in Spain, but I believe the number to be around 15. They are engaged in church planting ministries in various places and I have no way of giving specific information concerning their results.

The total number of missionaries involved in this grouping (primarily in church planting) is about 175.

North American Agencies (Service Organizations)

The organizations listed under this heading are those which are not specifically oriented to planting churches. They exist to help other groups through a specialized service.

The Billy Graham Association

The Billy Graham Association has one couple working with
the churches in the ministry of films. In the past three years
cooperating with churches and various groups in Spain, they
have succeeded in renting theaters in many villages and cities.
Offering a chance to see the films free, they have succeeded in
filling these theaters night after night to see such films as
"The Restless Ones." In the past two years they have cooper-
ated with the Pocket Testament League and given out Gospels
at the meetings as well as cards for a correspondence course.
The success in numbers of people who have come out to an
Evangelical meeting for the first time have been good. Many
have continued with the courses and they are being followed up
by Evangelism in Action.

Christian Literature Crusade (The Indiana, not the Pennsylvania group)

My information is that this group has sent twelve young
people for a two year effort in the Seville area in conjunction
with the Brethren Assemblies there.

Inter-Varsity Fellowship

Working with university students in the Barcelona area and
helping in youth retreats is the emphasis at present of I.V.F.
There was a single fellow in Madrid for awhile, but I believe
that he has since left.

Navigators

This is a new work in Spain and is centered in Madrid with
a work among university students. One couple represents the
agency and the work is not widely known at present.

Operation Mobilization

An organization which has been extremely active in Spain
for a number of years now. They have had large summer teams
working in the various areas of the country each year selling
books and distributing literature. Usually one or two teams
have been around on a yearly basis and have been helpful to
local churches in visitation programs. Now centered in Barcelona, and with a Spanish director, it has been zeroing in on a

particular area each summer with a saturation type program. It
has also become more concerned with church planting than it was
in the beginning. One team was kept in Granada long enough to
establish a church, and they were instrumental in helping a
mission with the formation of a church in Madrid. They have
overcome a good bit of the suspicion of the Spanish pastors of
earlier years and are now generally well received.

Pocket Testament League

Although the P.T.L. has had teams visiting in Spain over
the years, it has just recently assigned a couple there full
time. Teaming up with the Billy Graham Association worker,
they have distributed a good many Gospels at film showings in
rented theaters. They have also held meetings in several of
the churches and emphasized the need of Scripture distribution.

Youth With a Mission

A group with a strong emphasis on witness that has, up
until this past year, sent in summer teams to work wherever and
however possible. They have tried to cooperate with an established church and are excellent in street meetings and door-to-
door visitation. This past year they have assigned a couple
to work in Spain on a year-round basis and to coordinate the
teams of summer workers.

North American Agencies
Which Support Only Spanish Personnel

Under this heading I will list only the organizations which
have no foreign personnel in Spain, but do help in the support
of nationals. No information is given of their work. Some,
by their name, will reveal the type work, others will not. It
is hoped that the listing will be of help to those interested
in knowing the groups represented in Spain.

Campus Crusade for Christ International
Christian Literature Crusade
Churches of Christ
Church of God
Mennonite Board of Missions and Charities
Transworld Radio
World Gospel Crusades
World Home Bible League
Elim Missionary Assemblies

According to my information, there were a total of 234 (including wives) foreign missionaries working in Spain in 1972, representing 54 mission agencies. This figure is not exact to the person, but is reasonably close. To say that there are around 250 as a round figure would be a reasonable guess, and easier to remember. It is of interest to note that at least 75 per cent of these missionaries have been in Spain less than five years. In one sense, the country of Spain presents a pioneer field in spite of a history of over one hundred years of missionary efforts.

Foreign Missionaries and the Law

The missionary in Spain encounters fewer legal problems than would be expected in a country that has been so opposed to foreign influence in the past. The fact is that it is one of the easiest countries in the world to enter and this has presented other problems. Not only do the responsible organizations send in workers, but the cults have also entered. There is confusion in the minds of entering missionaries who are used to religious liberty in the "American" understanding of the word. This can lead to trouble very quickly as Arthur Blisset recently found out. The Spanish are very understanding people, but they do have certain laws. These laws can be followed with very successful results, but they do call for some understanding on the part of the missionary. I believe that it behooves every missionary in Spain to be familiar with the laws so that he is sure of what he can and cannot legally do. It is surprising how much can be done if you will only follow the rules. I am passing on some information that will be helpful in this respect. It was made available to the Evangelical Foreign Missions Consultation Committee by the *Servicio Evangélico de Asistencia Legal* and describes the legal position of foreign workers in Spain.

Legal Status of Foreigners
Under the Spanish Religious Liberty Law 44/67.

1. Foreigners have the same rights as the Spaniards in regards to religious liberty of worship and Christian testimony.
2. Foreigners may be recognized as ministers by the Confessional Associations to which they belong as long as these are inscribed to the Law.

3. Foreigners may constitute and legalize *Confessional
    Associations for evangelistic purposes and establish
    centers for the preaching of the Gospel, as long as the
    following requirements are observed:
    a) If the *Confessional Association is for foreigners
        and in a foreign language, they may constitute it
        with a minimum of three foreigners which represent
        it and with legal residence in Spain.
    b) If the *Confessional Association is for Spaniards
        but promoted by foreigners, these may represent it
        legally as long as there are no Spanish members.
        However, when the group or association has Spanish
        members, it must give the representation to the
        Spaniards or it cannot be considered a Spanish
        association.
4. Foreigners that enter Spain with a tourist passport cannot
    exercise any type of business with publications of any
    kind and, though they may give away literature, they can-
    not make money or business from it. (This includes the
    receiving of "donations" from material "given" away. It
    is necessary for one who does house-to-house colportage
    work to obtain a *Vendedor Ambulante* permit from local
    town hall.)
5. Foreigners with tourist passport (that is, without legal
    residence in Spain) cannot take part in public campaigns
    or meetings in public places or streets, nor carry bill-
    boards, play musical instruments, nor speak in public
    thoroughfares proclaiming any political, social or reli-
    gious ideal.
6. Foreigners with tourist passport (that is, without legal
    residence in Spain) may participate in public services if
    they are invited to speak or give lectures in churches or
    in halls previously authorized for such conference.

    It will be noticed at once that it is of utmost importance
for the missionary to become a resident of the country before
attempting to do any type of public ministry. This is where the
most trouble is likely to occur. Impatience on the part of
some can make for a good many problems on the part of all the
rest. Since it is not difficult to become a resident of Spain,

---

*By "Confessional Association" it is meant, "churches" or
"religious organization."

there is no excuse for a missionary not complying with the law. Compliance with the law can lead to a very fruitful and happy experience as a missionary in Spain.

There are other areas of interest which should be understood by those working in Spain. These are the various organizations within the Catholic Church. Becoming familiar with the official organs as well as the less conspicuous means of disseminating their ideas can be useful information. A glance through the magazine ¿Qué Pasa? from time to time will give an idea of the hard line, conservative church view, while Ecclesia would be more in the middle of the road line. It is not necessary to read these publications or others on a regular basis, but they should not be ignored either. It is always helpful to know what the people you are dealing with are reading.

Opus Dei

There is one Catholic organization which should be familiar to all missionaries in Spain. It is the Catholic lay organization Opus Dei (The Work of God). Founded by Jose Maria Escriva in 1928, The Work of God was designed to counteract the anticlericalism and secularism of the intellectual class as well as the increase of Marxist ideology. Forced into exile in France during the Civil War, Opus Dei began afresh in the 1940's. It was approved by the Holy See in 1950 as a "secular institute." That status has since been changed because of various pressures within the Church, but the power of Opus Dei continues to grow. Today it is one of the most powerful forces within the Catholic Church, and possibly the most powerful in Spain. Moving more by persuasion rather than force, it has infiltrated all levels of the social structure. Its daily newspapers and magazines combine with its bookstores, schools, and plush residences in making their mark in the country. It has been reported that there is scarcely a university professor that is not a member of the organization. It is the money and brains of Spain and thus has for natural enemies the Falangists, Catholic Action, and the Jesuits.

Most of the top bank officials, the leading businessmen. and the high-ranking military officers are Opus Dei men. When the shuffle came in Franco's Cabinet in 1969, he turned to Opus Dei for his replacements. Ten of the twenty places in the new Cabinet were filled by men who were either members or were

aligned with *Opus Dei*. The Falangists immediately protested
the *"Opus Dei coup d'etat"*, but could do nothing. They did
have a brief riot in Madrid when the news of the changes was
announced but nothing serious (Newsweek, November 10, 1969:59).
There is no doubt that Spain's economic recovery and progressive
attitudes of the past few years have been the result of the
"technocrats" of *Opus Dei*.

Although the organization claims to have no bias against
non-Catholics, it has been instrumental in the behind-the-scenes
activities to curtail the progress of the Protestants. This was
done in the area of radio broadcasting by the Evangelicals when
the Law of Religious Liberty was first passed. Of course this
cannot be proven as the methods used are the usual practice of
Opus. It is done by members acting as individuals; that way the
organization can deny any connection with the action. The worker
in Spain needs to be aware of *Opus Dei* and recognize its power.

Missionaries in Spain should also be students of the Spanish
culture. Knowing what changes are taking place in the society
can be helpful in relating the Gospel in terms that are meaning-
ful to the people. Care should be exercised that false conclusions are not arrived at by considering the rapid technological
changes as necessarily indicative of deeper sociological changes.
For example, it would be a mistake to assume that because the
majority of the people do not attend church that they have become less devoted to the Virgin Mary. Some practices in the life
of the people go deeper than mere conformity to church doctrines.

One of the outstanding characteristics of the Spanish culture is its deep devotion to the Virgin Mary. Every village has
its *"patrona"* and she is carefully looked after, often in great
luxury. Many of the "Virgins" have strong followings on the
international level and rivalries have even developed among
their followers. That a normally antichurch, anticlerical person will respond with great emotion to defend the Virgin is a
common occurance. During Holy Week, as the floats depicting
the last week in the life of Christ are carried through the
streets, it is always the float of the Virgin which receives
the greatest response. "She is greeted as a living person, a
blend of queen and popular singer" (Michener 1968:266). Why
should this be? It is because to the Spaniard she is not just
a symbol of their religion, she is part of their everyday life.
After all, it is the Virgin who has watched over their village
and families for centuries.

A westerner is sometimes puzzled by the picture of Mary and the infant Jesus. More often than not in a Latin country, it is with a bare breast. This is a most natural way of thinking of Mary as the symbolic "mother" in a mother-oriented society. It is the mother who is loyal and faithful to the family. It is she who bridges the gap between the children and the father. She often mediates in their behalf with the authoritarian father, obtaining for them the favors they dare not ask for in person. Thus she is the emotional center of the family world.

Over against this, the father is traditionally more or less expected to be unfaithful to his wife. He is often gone from the home and when he is there, he is the domineering head of the house. It is in the comparison of the family relationships with the religious counterparts that gives the understanding of the strong following of Mary. God is the substitute father, a judge and ruler. Christ is the suffering, dying one, which does not elicit an emotional attachment for healthy-minded people. Who wants to identify with death? Mary, on the other hand, is a symbol of life, beauty, and material benefits, someone with whom you want to identify. (Nida 1972:130-31).

There are many more items which probably should be dealt with that I have overlooked. As this is not a handbook for workers in Spain, I have only mentioned areas that I consider important and which need a more thorough treatment. I trust those who read this will be stimulated to think of ways in which the Protestant Church can be strengthened in the days ahead. It is my personal and sincere belief that we stand on the threshold of a great ingathering if we are faithful servants as God desires us to be.

CONCLUSION

Now that I have tried to give an up-to-date description of
the Protestants in Spain, the inevitable question is, what now?
How does the future look and what will be done? At this point,
it would be wonderful to be able to speak with authority and
give a detailed, infallible plan for church growth in Spain.
Unfortunately, no such plan exists. The situation is too complex and important for simplistic, superficial answers.

Much depends upon the future attitude of the Spanish government. At the very moment that I am writing these words
there has been a period of tighter controls. Recently a church
was refused approval of building plans, and there have been
problems for some missionaries in obtaining resident permits.
This, combined with the elimination of Evangelical radio programs, has given cause for some concern. Is it a temporary
restriction? What does it all mean? Who is behind it? These
are questions that beg to be answered.

Regardless of the political situation, there is still a
tremendous job to be done. Even if we assume that twenty-five
per cent of the population is faithful in its Catholic belief
and that another one per cent are non-Catholics of one sort or
another, there are still twenty-four and a half million people
that must be confronted with the Gospel in a vast "inner mission"
which neither Protestant nor Catholic is planning to launch.
These millions present the immediate and urgent responsibility

of the Evangelical Church in Spain. Hard, bold plans must be
laid for the evangelization of the nation. Nothing less will
suffice.

Above all, there is a need for further research. Drastic
gaps exist in figures and details concerning the existing
church. These statistics need to be sought out and recorded
for the benefit of all. Social, ethnic, economic, and geographical breakdowns are needed along with graphs for compar-
isons. Areas of growth need to be pinpointed and the reasons
for that growth examined. Guesses as to what has happened are
not enough. Hard facts are needed if definite plans are to be
laid. The Evangelical growth of thirty-three per cent over the
past decade is not a true indication of what can and must be
done in the future. That figure could be raised to at least
ten per cent per annum immediately. In order to do this, there
will have to be goals set, plans made, and God's Word obeyed.
Prayerful evaluations of present programs must be made to see
if they are really contributing to the growth of the Church, or
sapping vital strength. Missions and churches will have to
combine forces and move together in faith to accomplish the
task. There needs to be the conviction that it is God's will
and that He will provide. Only then will it be done.

The Evangelical Church will have to face up to and win the
cities. By 1960 forty-five per cent of the population of Spain
had become urban with twenty-seven per cent of the people living
in cities of more than 100,000. The government land-reform
plans of the 1960's are sure to have increased that number drastically. This means that there are now literally thousands of
socially dislocated people living in urban areas. Such people
should be receptive to the Gospel. Who has a plan for reaching
them? Studies of the cities will indicate *barrios* of recent
emigrants that are ripe for the harvest and are yet unharvested.
If the cities are not won, all will be lost. It is an irony
that the missionary and national pastors have to look to the
secular specialists to find out the religious trends of a country.
Should they not be the first to know?

It is vitally important to locate, identify, and evangelize
responsive peoples. That many such responsive subpopulations
exist is all too evident, as we examine the growth of the cults
such as the Jehovah's Witnesses. These "Johnny come latelies"
on the Spanish scene have, in a very short time, outstripped all

the Evangelicals combined. In spite of much opposition, doctrines that are negative (and run contrary to the Spanish mind),
they have made astounding progress. How do they do it? What
is the secret of their success? Actually, it is not a secret.
A quick glance through the yearbooks of the Witnesses gives us
a clue to the answer. Their careful tabulation of calls made
and Bible studies conducted in the homes, among other details,
reveals that they are an intensely active group. They do not
sit idly by, waiting for people to come to them. They go out
and find them. The Evangelicals must also be alert, active,
and effective in finding and winning the responsive.

One question that is continually raised is, "How are the
Pentecostals doing in Spain?". Their rapid growth in Latin
America has aroused much interest and the natural desire to
know if this is just a phenomenon particular to that area of
the world. I have usually brushed the question aside, saying
that Spain is different and that the Pentecostals have not
enjoyed very much success there. It came as a surprise to me
when doing the chart on page 85 to find that the number of
Pentecostal meeting places had risen from 3.7 per cent of the
total in 1961 to 29.5 per cent in 1971. One of the drawbacks
of this study has been the lack of specific figures on the
actual memberships of the various groups. I have, therefore,
resorted to using the number of meeting places as a guide to
size, which is not altogether satisfactory. For that reason, I
cannot give a definite answer as to whether the growth of any
group is real or not. A good bit of the growth, about one fourth,
among the Pentecostals can be attributed to the Gypsy Movement
of the past five or six years, but that is not the whole picture.
The very lack of this kind of information points out the need
for continued research and the compilation of the facts concerning the progress of the Protestants in Spain.

Throughout the study, and especially in Chapter IV, I have
made suggestions and raised questions for my co-workers in Spain
to consider. This I have done in love because of my desire that
the Evangelical Church move forward. Who knows but what has
happened already in Latin America - where Evangelicals have set
the pace even for the Roman Church - may be the most significant
way found in Spain as well. Millions of souls are at stake, as
we have seen.

APPENDICES

Appendix A

Key provisions of the 1953 Concordat between
the Holy See and the Spanish Government

In the Name of the Most Holy Trinity

The Apostolic Holy See and the Spanish State moved by the
desire to secure a fruitful cooperation for the greater good of
the religious and civil life of the Spanish nation, have decided to enter into a concordat. . .

ART. I. The Catholic Apostolic Roman religion will continue to be the sole religion of the Spanish nation and will
enjoy the rights and prerogatives which are due it in conformity with the Divine Law and the Canon Law.

ART. II. The Spanish State recognizes in the Catholic
Church its character of a perfect society, and guarantees it
the free and full exercise of its spiritual power as well as
of its jurisdiction. It also guarantees the free and public
worship of the Catholic religion. . .

ART. III. 1. The Spanish State recognizes the juridical
international status of the Holy See and the Vatican State.
2. In order to maintain in the traditional manner the friend-
ly relations between the Holy See and the Spanish State, a
Spanish ambassador to the Holy See, and an Apostolic Nuncio in
Madrid, will continue to be permanently accredited in their
respective posts. The Nuncio will be the dean of the diplomatic
corps according to the rules set by traditional law.

ART. V. The State will have as holy days those established
by the Church in the Code of Canon Law or in other particular
regulations on local festivities, the State will also provide
in its legislation the necessary facilities so that the faithful may comply during those days with their religious duties.

Civil authorities, both national and local, will see to
it that these days are duly observed.

ART. VI. According to the concession of Popes Pius V and
Gregory XIII, the Spanish priests will say daily prayers for
Spain and for the Chief of State, according to the traditional
form and the prescriptions of the Sacred Liturgy.

ART. VII. For the appointment of the resident Archbishops
and Bishops and their Coadjutors with the right of succession,
will continue in force the rules of the agreement stipulated
between the Holy See and the Spanish Government on June 7, 1941.
(This means that when any vacancy occurs, the government, in

consultation with the papal nuncio, submits six names to the
Pope, who in turn selects three of these names from which the
Spanish government finally picks the person actually designated
as Archbishop or Bishop.)

ART. IX. 2. In the establishment of a new diocese or
ecclesiastical province, and in other changes in the diocesan
boundaries which may be deemed necessary, the Holy See will
seek firt the agreement of the Spanish Government, unless the
changes are of minor importance. 3. The Spanish State binds
itself to provide the economic necessities of the diocese which
will be established in the future, by increasing accordingly
the funds established in Article XIX.

The Spanish State, also, per se, or through the local
interested corporations, will contribute an extraordinary sub-
sidy for initial expenses needed to organize the new dioceses;
in particular, it will subsidize the construction of new
cathedrals and those buildings necessary for the residence of
the prelate, officers of the chancery, and diocesan seminaries.

ART. XVI. 1. Prelates referred to in paragraph 2 of
Canon 120 of the Code of Canon Law may not be summoned before
a lay judge without having first obtained the required permission of the Holy See. 2. The Holy See agrees that liti-
gation on ownership or temporal rights in which clergymen and
members of religious orders are involved may be processed before Civil tribunals. In such cases, the Ordinary (Bishops)
concerned should receive prior notification of the place of
the trial, and also be informed of the court's decision on the
same day it is handed down. 3. The State recognizes and
respects the special authority of the tribunals of the Church
in matters relating to crimes which exclusively violate an
ecclesiastical law, in accordance with Canon 2, 198 of the
Code of Canon Law.

No appeal from sentences passed by these tribunals may be
brought before civil courts.

The Holy See agrees that cases against clergymen or other
members of religious orders involving other, non-canonical
crimes, which are covered by the penal laws of the State, may
be judged by the tribunals of the State. Nevertheless, the
judicial authority, before proceeding, should request, without
prejudice to precautionary measures to be taken in the case,
and with due reservation, the consent of the Ordinary concerned.
In the event that the latter, for serious reasons, believes it
his duty to deny such consent, he will communicate in writing
to the competent civil authority.

The necessary precautions will be taken to avoid all
publicity during the course of lawsuits concerning ecclesi-
astics. The findings of the case, as well as the verdict, in
the first as well as the last instance, shall be made known
to the Ordinary mentioned above. 5. In case of detention or
arrest, clergymen and members of religious orders shall be
treated with the consideration due their position and rank.
Sentences involving incarceration shall be served in ecclesi-
astic or religious institutions which, in the judgement of the
Ordinary concerned and of the state judicial authority, comply
with the guarantees required, or, at least, in institutions
other than secular, unless the competent ecclesiastical
authority shall have reduced the prisoner to the law status.
The rights of conditional liberty and other rights established
under state law shall be applicable to imprisioned clergy.

ART. XIX. 1. The Church and the State shall study by
common agreement means of creating an adequate church fund
which will provide for the maintenance of the clergy and of
religious activities. 2. Meanwhile, the State, by way of
idemification for past confiscations of church property, and
as a contribution to the Church's work for the good of the
nation, will provide the Church with an annual endowment.
This will include, in particular, the apportionment of funds
for diocesan Archbishops and Bishops, coadjutors, auxiliaries,
general vicariates, cathedral chapters, collegiate churches,
and parishes, as well as funds for seminaries and ecclesiastical
universities and for the general practice of the Catholic
religion. . .

If, in the future, a marked change in the general economic
situation should occur, the endowments will be adjusted to the
new situation in such a manner that support of religion and the
clergy will always be assured.

3. The State, ever faithful to the national tradition, will
reward annual subsidies for the construction and repair of
parish churches, rectories, and seminaries; the development of
religious orders, congregations and church institutions devoted
to missionary activities; and to care for monasteries of
historical value to Spain. It will also award subsidies toward
the support of the Colegio Español de San José and the Spanish
Church residence of Montserrat in Rome. 4. The State will col-
laborate with the Church in establishing and financing social
institutions for the benefit of aged, feeble and invalid clergymen; also, the State will provide an adequate pension to

resident Prelates who, for the reasons of age or health, retire from their posts.

ART. XXIII. The Spanish State recognizes the full civil validity of marriages performed according to the norms of Canon Law.

ART. XXIV. 1. The Spanish State recognizes the exclusive competence of the ecclesiastical courts in cases involving the nullity of ecclesiastical marriage, in those where separation is sought, or in other cases involving the dispensation from marriages <u>ratum non consummatun</u> or having to do with the Pauline privilege. 2. On ce a demand of separation of of nullity has been established and admitted before the ecclesiastical tribunal, the civil court should dictate, at the request of the interestes party, both precautionary norms and measures used to regulate the civil effects of the pending process. 3. When its sentences and decisions have been confirmed and have become enforcible, the ecclesiastical courts will notify the civil courts in its jurisdiction. The civil court, in turn, will decree the necessary court's decisions. The civil court will ordain, in the case of nullity, the <u>super rato</u> dispensations, or the application of the Pauline privilege, all these measures to be duly noted in the Civil Registry on the margin of the marriage certificate. 4. In general all sentences, decrees, and decisions of an administrative nature issued by ecclesiastical authorities regarding any of the matters subject to their jurisdiction will have validity also in the civil court. Once they have been notified, the state authorities and civil officials will render the necessary assistance in carrying out these sentences, decisions and decrees.

ART. XXVI. In all institutions of learning--whatever their level and purpose and whether belonging to the State or not---education will be imparted in accordance with the dogmatic and moral principles of the Catholic Church.

Ordinaries will freely exercise their mission of vigilance regarding the integrity of faith, good morals and religious teaching in these educational institutions.

Ordinaries may demand the banning and suppression of textbooks, publications and other teaching material which are contrary to Catholic dogma and morals.

ART. XXVII. . The Spanish State guarantees the teaching of the Catholic religion as a regular and compulsory subject in all educational institutions, whether state-controlled or not, and whatever their level and purpose. Children of non-Catholic parents will be exempt from this teaching, upon the request of

resident prelates who, for reasons of age or health, retire
from their posts.

ART. XXIII. The Spanish State recognizes the full civil
validity of marriages performed according to the norms of
Canon Law.

ART. XXIV. 1. The Spanish State recognizes the exclusive
competence of the ecclesiastical courts in cases involving the
nullity of ecclesiastical marriage, in those where separation
is sought, or in other cases involving the dispensation from
marriages ratum non consummatun or having to do with the
Pauline privilege. 2. Once a demand of separation or of
nullity has been established and admitted before the ecclesiastical tribunal, the civil court shoul dictate, at the request of the interested party, both precautionary norms and
measures used to regulate the civil effects of the pending
process. 3. When its sentences and decisions have been confirmed and have become enforcible. the ecclesiastical courts
will notify the civil courts in its jurisdiction. The civil
court, in turn, will decree the necessary court's decisions.
The civil court will ordain, in the case of nullity, the super
rato dispensations, or the application of the Pauline privilege, all these measures to be duly noted in the Civil
Registry on the margin of the marriage certificate. 4. In
general all sentences, decrees, and decisions of an administrative nature issued by ecclesiastical authorities regarding any
of the matters subject to their jurisdiction will have validity
also in the civil court. Once they have been notified, the
state authorities and civil officials will render the necessary
assistance in carrying out these sentences, decisions and
decrees.

ART. XXVI. In all institutions of learning--whatever
their level and purpose and whether belonging to the State or
not--education will be imparted in accordance with the dogmatic and moral principles of the Catholic Church.

Ordinaries will freely exercise their mission of vigilance
regarding the integrity of faith, good morals and religious
teaching in these educational institutions.

Ordinaries may demand the banning and suppression of textbooks, publications and other teaching materials which are
contrary to Catholic dogma and morals.

ART. XXVII. 1. The Spanish State guarantees the teaching
of the Catholic religion as a regular and compulsory subject in
all educational institutions, whether state controlled or not,
and whatever their level and purpose. Children of non-Catholic
parents will be exempt from this teaching, upon the request of

their parents or tutors. 2. In primary public schools,
teachers themselves will impart religious instruction, except
when the Ordinary objects to someone for reasons prescribed in
Canon 1381, Article 3, of the Code of Canon Law. This instruction also will be periodically supplemented by Cathechism
lessons given by the parish priest or his delegate. 3. In
public institutions of secondary education, religious instruction will be given by priests or religious, or instead by law
professors appointed by the competent civil authorities on recommendations of the Diocesan Ordinary. . . 7. Professors of
religion at non-state schools must have a certificate of
aptitude issued by the Ordinary. Revocation of this certificate
will instantly deprive the teacher of his functions. 8. The
subject matter of courses in religion, both in public and non-
public schools, will be prepared in accordance with the compr-
tent ecclesiastical authority. Only textbooks approved by the
ecclesiastical authority can be used in the teaching of religion.

ART. XXVIII. 1. State universities may impart by agreement with the ecclesiastical authorities, regular courses
specializing in Scholastic Philosophy, Sacred Theology and
Canon Law programs and textbooks should be approved by the
same ecclesiastical authorities. These courses may be given
by priests, religious or lay teachers holding graduate degrees
from a Catholic university, or the equivalent from the respective
Order when a member of a religious order is concerned; all of
them must have the Nihil Obstat of the diocesan Ordinary.

ART. XXIX. The State will assure that services and
institutions which mold public opinion, and in particular
radio and television, grant due attention to the explaination
and defense of the religious truths, a task which will be
trusted to priests and members of religious orders and in
accordance with the Ordinary.

ART. XXX. 1. . . . .The State will seek to render as much
financial help as possible to institutions of religious orders
and congregations, especially those devoted to the training of
missionaries.

ART. XXXI. 1. The Church freely exercises its right,
as established by Canon 1375 of the Code of Canon Law, to
organize and operate its own schools, regardless of level or
purpose, which are open for general registration-including lay
students. In matters regarding recognition by the State of
studies undertaken in such schools, Civil authorities will act
in agreement with the proper ecclesiastical authority.

ART. XXXII. 1. Religious care in the armed forces will
conform to the regulations established by the agreement of
August 5, 1950.

ART. XXXIII. 1. The State, in agreement with the ecclesiastical authority, will provide the necessary means so that
hospitals, sanitaria, penal establishments, orphanages and
like institutions shall have the proper religious assistance
for their inmates and the personnel in charge. By the same
token, the State will seek the observance of these norms in
similar establishments in private hands.

FINAL PROTOCOL. At the time of signing the Concordat,
which is today being entered into between the Holy See and
Spain, the plenipotentiaries signing the agreement have, by
mutual agreement, made the following statements which will be
an integral part of the Concordat itself:. . .

In Reference to Article I

In regard to the toleration of non-Catholic faith, in
territories under Spanish jurisdiction in Africa, the status
quo observed up to now will continue in force. . .

In Reference to Article XXIII

A. For recognition, by the State of civil effects of
canonical marriage, it will be sufficient for the marriage
certificate to be transcribed in the corresponding Civil
Registry. . .

(1) Under no circumstances shall the presence of a state
official during the celebration of a canonical marriage be
considered as a required condition for acknowledgment of its
civil effects. . .

C. In the matter of acknowledgment of a mixed marriage
between Catholic and non-Catholic persons, the State shall
formulate its legislation so as to harmonize with Canon Law. . .

Appendix B
PROTESTANT OCCUPATION BY PROVINCES

Region	Churches 1933	Churches 1961	Churches 1971	Population 1971
NEW CASTILE				
Cuidad Read	6	4	6	511,943
Madrid	9	18	32	3,703,119
Toledo	0	1	2	457,546
Guadalajara	0	0	0	146,862
Cuenca	0	0	2	244,797
OLD CASTILE				
Avila	4	2	3	204,727
Logroño	2	2	2	231,728
Santander	1	1	3	452,404
Valladolid	3	3	4	378,885
Burgos	0	3	3	342,003
Soria	0	0	0	116,908
Segovia	0	0	0	169,425
Palencia	0	1	2	207,318
LEON				
Zamora	3	3	7	253,084
León	3	2	7	554,109
Salamanca	1	3	3	365,646
EXTREMADURA				
Badajoz	2	3	3	704,849
Cáceres	1	2	2	468,310
GALICIA				
La Coruña	6	17	17	1,009,752
Lugo	4	5	3	427,595
Orense	1	6	7	426,132
Pontevedra	8	11	11	742,907
ASTURIAS				
Oviedo	2	11	13	1,030,719
BASQUE PROVINCES				
Guipuzcoa	1	3	4	642,075
Vicaya	1	2	5	1,052,417
Alava	0	0	3	196,996
NAVARRA				
Navarra	0	0	2	440,609
ARAGON				
Huesca	6	6	9	225,452
Zaragoza	2	5	6	721,400
Teruel	0	0	0	173,160

PROTESTANT OCCUPATION BY PROVINCES

Region	Churches 1933	Churches 1961	Churches 1971	Population
CATALONIA				
Barcelona	20	63	89	3,793,156
Gerone	5	7	6	408,584
Lérida	7	6	11	338,590
Tarragona	1	6	15	415,977
BALEARIC ISLANDS				
Baleares	6	7	13	517,012
VALENCIA				
Alicante	3	7	17	817,255
Castellon	1	2	4	379,168
Valencia	8	15	34	1,657,425
MURCIA				
Albacete	3	3	2	315,588
Murcia	9	9	15	825,788
ANDALUSIA				
Cádiz	8	10	17	396,103
Córdoba	2	1	4	733,387
Granada	2	2	7	707,351
Jaén	14	12	27	655,367
Málaga	6	9	7	804,456
Sevilla	4	10	12	1,421,570
Huelva	0	2	3	367,678
CANARY ISLANDS				
Las Palmas	0	3	11	574,932
Santa Cruz	0	5	17	603,451

(1933:Grubb & García   1961:Estruch   1971:Capó)

Appendix C

QUESTIONNAIRE SENT TO MISSIONARIES

I represent the_____

and have been working in Spain for _____years. I have also

worked in_____for_____years.

My work is in the area of (Evangelism) (Church Planting)
                          (Teaching) (   )

Our work consists of _____(Churches, groups) with

_____baptized believers. The work was begun in 19 ____.

College degree: Yes _____No_____Graduate work?_____years.

In what field is your degree?_____

In what way do you feel the foreign missionary can make the
greatest contribution to the work in Spain?_____

_____

_____

Do you feel that the possibilities of education for leaders in
the National Church are sufficient?_____yes _____no. Do you
have any suggestions for improving the situation?_____

_____

What do you feel are the greatest obstacles to church growth

in Spain?_____

Do you feel that the Religious Liberty Law has been helpful?___

Why?_____

Are records of your work kept, such as baptism etc. on a yearly
basis? If so would they be available for statistical purposes?
If no records are kept is there a person available with whom I
could talk who has an accurate knowledge of the work?
Their name and address please -

Appendix D

Nombre de la iglesia o grupo_____

Direción_____

Año de fundación_____¿por quién?_____

¿De cuál grupo es la iglesia miembro?_____

Número de miembros actualmente_____

El lugar de cultos es (Aquilado) (Propio) (Otro)

¿Recibe la iglesia ayuda del extranjero?_____

¿En qué forma?_____

Información de la miembresía

	1940-44	1945-49	1950-54	1955-59	1960-64	1965-70
No de Bautismos						
No de Translados						
No de Bajas						

Tiene Esc. dominical ____Asistencia promedio _____

Información pastoral

Nivel de educación (Primaria)(Bachillerato)(Universidad)(Seminario)

Años que lleva en el ministerio _____

Envie a: David Vought

BIBLIOGRAPHY

(This list is confined to sources consulted and references cited.)

ACEVES, Joseph B.
   1971   *Social Change in a Spanish Village.* Cambridge, Mass.,
          Schenkman Publishing Co., Inc.

ALAN, Ray
   1962   "Franco's Spain and the New Europe," *Commentary,*
          (September) 233-236.

ALBERTOS, José Luis
   1968   "Los No Católicos en España," *Mundo,* (6 de Julio)
          54-61.

ALEMANY, Luis Vich
   1970   *El Protestantism en Mallorca.* Palma de Mallorca.

AMERICA
   1964a   "Religious Liberty in Spain," *America,* (October 24)
           CXI 471.

   1964b   "Protestants in Spain; More Freedom," *America,*
           (March 7) CX 300-301.

ANONYMOUS
  1965   The Truth about the Protestant Situation in Spain.
          A tract written by an anonymous Spanish Christian,
          Wheaton, Ill., United Evangelical Action.

BABINGTON, John Albert
  1971   The Reformation. Port Washington, N. Y., Kennikat
          Press.

BARBANCHO, Alfonso G.
  1970   Las Migraciónes interiores españolas en 1961-1965.
          Madrid, Estudios del Instituto de Desarrollo
          Económica.

BLANCHARD, Paul
  1962   Freedom and Catholic Power in Spain. Boston, Beacon
          Press.

  1966   Paul Blanchard on Vatican II. Boston, Beacon Press.

BOEHMEN, Edward
  1965   Spanish Reformers of Two Centuries from 1520. 3 Vols.,
          New York, Burt Franklin.

BRAUN, Neil
  1971   Laity Mobilized; Reflections on Church Growth in
          Japan and Other Lands. Grand Rapids, Mich., William
          B. Eerdmans Publishing Co.

BRAVO, Luis E.
  1965   Diálogo con Protestantes. Madrid, Fe Católica.

BREMAN, Gerald
  1962   The Spanish Labyrinth. Cambridge, Cambridge Press.

BROWN, E. Stuart
  1964   The Trump of Jubilee. Parkstone, Vellum Samson
          Printers Ltd.

BROWNE, George
  1859   A History of the British and Foreign Bible Society
          1804-1854. Vol. II. London, Bagster & Sons.

BUSTOS, Felixberto G. ed.
  1934   New Philippines. Manila, Carmelo and Bauermann Inc.

CANCLINI, Santiago
1948   *Escritos de Pablo Besson, Tomo I.* Buenos Aires,
       Junto de Publicaciones de la Convención Evangélica
       Bautista.

CAPO, Humberto
1971   *Anuario Evangélica Española.* Proof sheets for the
       compilation of the annual of the location of the
       Evangelical churches in Spain. (Mimeographed.)

CARRILLO de ARBORNOZ, A. F.
1959   *Roman Catholicism and Religious Liberty.* Geneva,
       World Council of Churches.

1963   *The Basis of Religious Liberty.* New York, Associated
       Press.

CARTA CIRCULAR
1971   "Las Iglesias evangélicas ante su Vocación," *Carta
       Circular,* No. 219 (Enero-Febrero).

CASTRO, Adelfo de
1851   *Historia de los Protestantes españoles.* Cádiz,
       Imprinta, Librería, y Litografia de la Revista
       Médica.

CHRISTIAN CENTURY
1940   "The New Order in Spain," *Christian Century,*
       57:1332-3.

1962a "American Money and Spanish Tyranny," *Christian
       Century,* 79:76.

1962b "Signs of Hope in Spain," *Christian Century,* 79:402.

1963   "News of the Christian World," *Christian Century,*
       80:1527-1529.

1965   "Protestants, Catholics View Religious Liberty,"
       Christian Century, 82:788-790.

1972   "Church and State on Outs," *Christian Century,* 89:58.

CHRISTIANITY TODAY
1973   Vol. XVII, No. 10, 49-50.

CLARK, Frincis E., CLARK, Harriet A.
  1909   The Gospel in Latin Lands. New York, The MacMillan
          Co.

COMIN, Alfonso C.
  1966   España ¿País de Misión? Barcelona, Editorial Nova
          Terra.

COMMISSION
  1961   "Church Reopens at Seville," Commission, No. 3,24:
          89.

  1963.   "Permission Given for Notices," Commission,
          No. 11, 26:15.

  1964   "Court Upholds Church Right," Commission, No. 3,
          27:31.

CORNWALL, Richard
  1966   "The Changing Mood," America, (June 25).

CRIVILLE, Camilo
  1954   Pequeño Diccionario de las Sectas protestantes.
          Madrid, Editorial Apostolado de la Prensa S. A.

DELPECH, Jacques
  1956   The Oppression of Protestants in Spain. London,
          Lutterworth Press.

DENVER CATHOLIC REGISTER
  1965   "American Sects Spreading Propagands in Spain
          Despite Lack of Recognition," The Denver Catholic
          Register, (August 12).

DESUMBILA, José
  1964   El Ecumenismo en España. Barcelona, Editorial
          Estela, S. A.

DIAZ-PLAJA, Fernando
  1967   The Spaniard and the Seven Deadly Sins. New York,
          Charles Scribner's Sons. Translated from the Spanish
          by John Inderwick Palmer.

  1969   El Español y las siete Pecados capitales. Madrid,
          Alianza Editorial.

DRANE, James F.
1966   "The Changing Law," *America,* (June 25).

EL CIERVO
1958   No. 61, (Enero).

ESTRUCH, Juan
1967   *Los Protestantes españoles.* Barcelona, Editorial
        Nova Terra.

EVANS, Robert P.
1963   *Let Europe Hear.* Chicago, Moody Press.

FERNANDEZ, Gabino Campos
1972   Personal correspondence, May 5.

FERNSWORTH, Lawrence
1954   "New Concordat with Spain," *Christian Century*
        (May 26) 637-9.

FLORES, José
1969   "La Sociedad Bíblica en España," *Carta Circular,*
        No. 207, (Enero-Febrero).

FOY, Felician A. ed.
1972   *1972 Catholic Almanac.* Huntington, Ind., Our
        Sunday Visitor, Inc.

GARRISON, W. E.
1950   "Religious Liberty in Spain," *Christian Century,*
        67:1262-1265.

GARCIA, Arajuo C., GRUBB, Kenneth
1933   *Religion in the Republic of Spain.* London, World
        Dominion Press.

GARCIA, Zacarias Villada
1926   *Historia eclesiastica de España.* Tomo I, Primero
        Parte. Madrid, Compania Ibro-Americana de
        Publicaciones, S. A.

GIBSON, Jesse O. ed.
1972   *Seventh-day Adventist Yearbook 1972.* Washington,
        General Conference of Seventh-day Adventist.

GIL, Ruben
  1970   "¿Hace falta la evangelización en España?"
          Restauración, (Julio-Agosto).

GIRONELLA, José María
  1971   *100 Españoles y Dios*. Barcelona, Ediciones Nauta,
          S. A.

GOMEZ, Patricio
  1953   *Los Evangélicos españoles en la Historia*. A privately
          published pamphlet.

GOLDSTON, Robert
  1966   *The Civil War in Spain*. Greenwich, Conn., Fawcett
          Publishing, Inc.

GONZALEZ, Joan
  1969   *El Protestantisme a Catalunya*. Barcelona, Editorial
          Bruguera.

  1970   *Un Segle de Protestantisme a Catalunya*. Barcelona,
          Ediciones Evangéliques Europees.

GOODSPEED, Edgar J.
  1950   *The Apostolic Fathers*. New York, Harper & Brothers.

GRAYZEL, Solomon
  1970   "The Beginnings of Exclusion," *Jewish Quarterly
          Review*, Vol. 61.

GUTIERREZ, Arturo M.
  1963   *Albores del Cristianismo en España*. Levittown,
          Penna., Publicaciones Portavoz.

  1969   *El Campo de Gibraltar en la Obra evangélica española*.
          Barcelona, Ediciones Evangélicas Europeas.

HENRY, Carl F. H.
  1964   "Pressures on Spain for Protestant Rights,"
          Christianity Today, (April 10).

HERR, Richard
  1969   *The Eighteenth Century Revolution in Spain*.
          Princeton, N. J., Princeton University Press.

HOWARD, George P.
1944   "The Voice of Liberal Spain," *Christian Century*, 61:921-922.

HUGHEY, David J.
1955   *Religious Freedom in Spain*. London, The Carey Kingsgate Press, Ltd.

1964   *Historia de los Bautistas en España*. Barcelona, Imprinta Salvado. Translated from English by Juan Juan Lacue.

INSTITUTO NACIONAL DE ESTADISTICA
1971   *España-Anuario Estadístico*. Madrid, Imprenta Nacional del Boletín Oficial de Estado.

IRIZARRY, Carmen
1966   *The Thirty Thousand*. New York, Harcourt, Brace & World, Inc.

JANSSENS, Louis
1965   *Freedom of Conscience and Religious Freedom*. New York, Alba House.

JEHOVAH'S WITNESS
1962   *Yearbook of Jehovah's Witness*. New York, Watch Tower Bible and Tract Society of Pennsylvania.

1965   *Yearbook of Jehovah's Witness*. New York, Watch Tower Bible and Tract Society of Pennsylvania.

1967   *Yearbook of Jehovah's Witness*. New York, Watch Tower Bible and Tract Society of Pennsylvania.

1970   *Yearbook of Jehovah's Witness*. New York, Watch Tower Bible and Tract Society of Pennsylvania.

JIMENEZ, José Lozano
1966   *Meditacion española sobre la Libertad religiosa*. Barcelona, Editorial Destino.

JURJI, Edward J. ed.
1959   *The Ecumenical Era in Church and Society*. New York, The MacMillan Co.

KAMEN, Henry
    1965   The Spanish Inquisition. New York, Mentor Books.

KELLER, Adolf
    1927   Protestant Europe: Its Crisis and Outlook. London,
            Hodder and Stoughton.

    1942   Christian Europe Today. New York, Harper & Brothers
            Publishers.

KENSIT
    1931   Spain's New Day - An Account of Mr. Kensit's Recent
            Tour. London, Protestant Truth Society.

KLAIBER, Jeffrey L.
    1970   "Pentecostal Breakthrough," America, (January 31).

KUNG, Hans, CONGAR, Yeves, & O'HARE, Daniel eds.
    1964   Council Speeches of Vatican II. Glen Rock, N. J.,
            Paulist Press.

LATOURETTE, Kenneth Scott
    1953   A History of Christianity. New York, Harper & Row,
            Publishers.

    1971   A History of the Expansion of Christianity Vol. 1
            Grand Rapids. Mich., Zondervan Publishing House.

LEA, Henry Charles
    1906-8 A History of the Inquisition of Spain. 4 Vols.

    1967   Religious History of Spain. New York, Burt Franklin

LLORENT, Juan A.
    1967a   A Critical History of the Inquisition of Spain.
            Williamstown, Mass., The John Lilburne Co. Publisher.

    1967b   La Inquisición y los Españoles. Madrid, Editorial
            Ciencia Nueva.

LLORENT, Miguel de la Pinta
    1948   La Inquisicion española. Madrid, Archivo Agustiniano.

    1949   Las Cárceles inquisitorials españolas. Madrid, Archivo
            Agustiniano.

LONGBUTTON, H. D.
 1931   *What I Saw in Spain*. Liverpool, Handly Brothers, Ltd.

LOPEZ, Eduardo Ramos
 1971   "Los Españoles en el Extranjero," *Los Domingos de
        ABC*, (12 de Septiembre).

LORD, David
 1940   "The Coming Spanish Reformation," *Christian Century*,
        57:604-606.

LUZBETAK, Louis J.
 1970   *The Church and Cultures*. Techny, Ill., Diving Word
        Publications.

MANANON, Gregorio
 1964   *The Liberal in the Looking Glass*. New York, Long
        House Publishing, Inc.

MATTHEWS, Herbert L.
 1957   *The York and the Arrows*. New York, George Braziller,
        Inc.

MCCRIE, Thomas
 1842   *Reformation in Spain*. Philadelphia, Presbyterian
        Board of Publishers.

MC GAVRAN, Donald A.
 1970   *Understanding Church Growth*. Grand Rapids, Mich.,
        William B. Eerdmans Publishing Co.

MENENDEZ Y PELAYO, M.
 1956   *Historia de los Heterodoxos españoles*. 2 Vols.
        Madrid, Biblioteca de Autores Cristianos.

MENENDEZ, Ramón Pidal
 1966   *The Spaniards in Their History*. New York, W. A.
        Norton & Co.

MEYRICK, Frederick
 1892   *The Church in Spain*. London, Wells Gardner, Darton
        & Co.

MACKAY, John A.
 1933   *The Other Spanish Christ*. New York, The MacMillan Co.

MICHENER, James A.
   1968   *Iberia*. New York, Random House, Inc.

MILLER, Townsand
   1963   *The Castles and the Crown*. New York, Coward-McCann,
           Inc.

MONROY, Juan A.
   1958   *Defensa de los Protestantes españoles*. Tanger,
           Ediciones Luz y Verdad.

   1967   *Libertad religiosa y Ecumenismo*. Madrid, Editorial
           Irmayol.

   1971   "El porque de los Concordatos," *Restauración*,
           (Abril) 4-5.

   1972a   "Los Debates en la Cortes," *Restauración*, (Julio-
           Agosto) 20.

   1972b   "Definitivamente aprobada," *Restauración*, (Julio-
           Agosto) 25.

MORENO, Antonio Montero
   1961   *La Persecución religiosa en España. 1936-1939*.
           Madrid, Biblioteca de Autores Cristianos.

MOURRET, Fernando & THOMPSON, Newton
   1946   *History of the Catholic Church*. Vol 1. St. Louis,
           B. Herder Book Co.

MUÑOZ. Jesús
   1964   *Libertad Reliaiosa*. Comillas, Universidad Pontifica.

MC NASPY. C. J.
   1967   "The Change in Spain," *America*. (July 29).

NEWSWEEK
   1963   "Delicate Matter; Broader Rights for Protestants,"
           Newsweek, 61:78.

   1969   "The Succession." *Newsweek*, 67:59.

   1971   "Turnabout in Spain," *Newsweek*. 69:102.

NIDA, Eugene A.
  1957   "The Roman Catholic. Communist, and Protestant
          Approach to Social Structure," *Practical Anthro-
          pology*, 4:209-219.

  1972   *Message and Mission*. South Pasadena. Calif.,
          William Carey Library.

ORTS. Juan González
  1932   *El destino de los Pueblos Ibericos*. Madrid,
          Librería Nacional Y Extranjera.

PETERS, George W.
  1970   *Saturation Evangelism*. Grand Rapids, Mich.,
          Zondervan Publishing House.

PITT-RIVERS, Julian A.
  1971   *The People of the Sierra*. Chicago, The University
          of Chicago Press.

PORTAVOZ
  1972   "Así estan las cifras estadísticas de la situación
          religiosa no católica en España,"
          (Febrero) 23:20.

POVEDA, Luis ed.
  1965   *II Conferencia Nacional de Obreros evangélicos*.
          Madrid. Minutes of the conference held in Madrid
          from the 6-8th of October 1965.

RIDRUEJO, Dionisio
  1963   "Spain's Restless Voices," *Catholic World*, (May)
          88-94.

ROE, James M.
  1965   *A History of the British and Foreign Bible Society.
          1905-1954*. London, British and Foreign Bible Society.

SALADRIGAS, Robert
  1971   *Las Confesiones no católicas en España*. Barcelona,
          Ediciones del Bolsillo.

SEGARRA, Francisco
  1966   *La Libertad Religiosa*. Barcelona, TIP. CAT. Casals.

SEVENTH-DAY ADVENTIST
  1935   *Yearbooks of the Seventh-day Adventist Denomination.*
  to   Washington, General Conference of Seventh-day
  1970   Adventist.

SMALLEY, William A.
  1967   *Readings in Missionary Anthropology.* Tarrytown,
           N. Y., Practical Anthropology.

STOUGHTON, John
  1883   *Memories of the Spanish Reformers.* London, The
           Religious Tract Society

SWOMLEY, John M. Jr.
  1966   "What Chance for Religious Freedom in Spain?"
           Christian Century, 83:663-664.

THOMAS, Hugh
  1962   *Spain.* New York, Time Inc.

TIME
  1963   "Emancipation in Spain," *Time*, 81:35.

  1966   "Troubled Citadel," *Time*, 84:65.

TORRUBIANO, Jaime Ripoll
  1931   *Política religiosa de Democracia española.*
           Madrid, Javier Morato

TRENCHARD, Ernest H.
  1930?   *Sketches from Missionary Life in Spain.* London.
           Marshall, Morgan & Scott Ltd.

TURBERVILLE, S. S.
  1968   *The Spanish Inquisition.* Archon Books.

VALBUENA, M.
  1965   "Hace un Siglo," *Edificación Cristiana*, Número
           especial misionero. (Agosto-Octubre).

VALL, Hector
  1971   "More Ecumenism in Spain," *Journal of Ecumenical
           Studies.* Vol. 8, 214-216.

VARETTO, Juan C.
  1959   *La Reforma religiosa del Siglo XVI.* Buenos Aires,
          Junta Bautista de Publicaciones.

VASSADY, Bela
  1965   *Christ's Church: Evangelical, Catholic, and Reformed.*
          Grand Rapids, Mich., William B. Eerdmans Publishing
          Co.

VIDAL, Daniel
  1968   *Nosotros los Protestantes españoles.* Madrid,
          Cuadernos y Ensayos Marova.

WAGNER, C. Peter
  1970   *Latin American Theology: Radical or Evangelical?*
          Grand Rapids, Mich., William B. Eerdmans Publishing
          Co.

  1973   *Look Out! The Pentecostals Are Coming.* Carol Stream,
          Ill., Creation House. Page numbers in this study
          were taken from the original manuscript and may differ
          from the book.

WATT, W. Montgomery
  1965   *A History of Islamic Spain.* Edinburgh, Edinburgh
          University Press.

WHITTEN, Nella Dean
  1961   "Castle for Christ in Spain," *Commission*, No. 11,
          24:325.

DAT⁻ DUE

ABOUT THE AUTHOR

Dale G. Vought was born in Johnson City, New York. In 1954 he graduated from Zephyrhills High School (Fla.) and entered the United States Air Force. Receiving an honorable discharge in 1958, he entered Columbia Bible College in Columbia, S. C., and in 1962 graduated with a B. A. in Biblical Education. While at Columbia he met and married Anne Blackstock and they now have a daughter, Christina. During 1962-63 Mr. Vought served as Youth Director for the First Baptist Church in Duxbury, Mass. Returning to Columbia Bible College in the summer of 1963, he served as Assistant to the Business Manager and completed his studies for the M.A. in Biblical Education in 1966. In December of 1965 he had accepted the responsibility for the Purchasing and Buildings Departments of The Evangelical Alliance Mission in Wheaton, Ill. and served in that capacity until leaving for the field of Spain in January 1968. During his term of service, Mr. Vought served as Field Chairman for two years.